CHRISTIAN THOUGHT REVISITED

CHRISTIAN THOUGHT REVISITED

Three Types of Theology

JUSTO L. GONZÁLEZ

ABINGDON PRESS
NASHVILLE

CHRISTIAN THOUGHT REVISITED:
THREE TYPES OF THEOLOGY

Library of Congress Cataloging-in-Publication Data

GONZALEZ, JUSTO L.
Christian thought revisited: three types of theology /
Justo L. González.
p.   cm. Bibliography: p.   Includes index.

ISBN 0-687-07629-3 (pbk.: alk. paper)

1. Theology, Doctrinal—History. 2. Theology—
Methodology—History. I. Title.
BT21.2.G59   1989   8-7390
230'.09—dc19   CIP

71180

Scripture quotations are from the Revised Standard Version of the Bible, copyright
1946, 1952, 1971 by the Division of Christian Education of the National Council of
Churches of Christ in the USA. Used by permission.

Notations designated ANF are from *Writings of the Ante-Nicene Fathers*, edited by
Alexander Roberts and James Donaldson; those designated NPNF are from *Writings of
the Nicene and Post-Nicene Fathers*—both published by the William B. Eerdmans
Publishing Co. *Luther's Works* (LW) were published by Fortress Press and by Concordia
Publishing House.

MANUFACTURED BY THE PARTHENON PRESS AT
NASHVILLE, TENNESSEE, UNITED STATES OF AMERICA

Wherefore I do also call upon thee, Lord God of Abraham, and God of Isaac, and God of Jacob and Israel, who art the Father of our Lord Jesus Christ, the God who, through the abundance of Thy mercy, hast had a favour towards us, that we should know Thee, who hast made heaven and earth, who rulest over all, who art the only and true God, above whom there is none other God; grant, by our Lord Jesus Christ, the governing power of thy Holy Spirit; give to every reader of this book to know Thee, that Thou art God alone.

—*A Prayer of Irenaeus*

Contents

Preface

The material in this book has evolved from many years of writing and lecturing on the history of Christian thought. It began to take its present shape in the early 1970s when I was teaching at Candler School of Theology. During those years, William B. Mallard and Manfred Hoffmann, with whom I was team-teaching, made helpful and encouraging comments.

Later I expanded this material for a course at the Interdenominational Theological Center, and since then I have used it in institutions of theological education and also in lectures to a number of congregations. It is the requests from such congregations for more information on the subject that have prompted me to put this material in writing.

Much credit goes to my wife, Catherine Gunsalus González, professor of church history at Columbia Theological Seminary, who encouraged me when various tasks and inclinations led me in other directions and who provided many valuable suggestions and corrections.

J.L.G.

List of Abbreviations

ACW	*Ancient Christian Writers*
ANF	*The Ante-Nicene Fathers* (Grand Rapids)
DTC	*Dictionnaire de Théologie Catholique*
JTS	*Journal of Theological Studies*
LW	*Luther's Works* (St. Louis; Philadelphia)
NPNF	*The Nicene and Post-Nicene Fathers* (Grand Rapids)
PG	*Patrologiae cursus completus . . . series Graeca* (ed. Migne)
PL	*Patrologiae cursus completus . . . series Latina* (ed. Migne)
RelSt	*Religious Studies*
Story	Justo L. González, *The Story of Christianity*
ZntW	*Zeitschrift für die neutestamentliche Wissenshaft*

Whenever possible I have quoted translations that are readily available, such as those in ANF, ACW, NPNF, and so on. Since parentheses and brackets appear often in such translations, I have marked my own additions and comments with braces—{ } —not with square brackets as is customary.

It is regrettable that most of these translations—often the only ones available to the public—are riddled with sexist language. The reader should note that most often this is the result of the translators' use of English and does not appear in the original Greek or Latin.

Introduction

"They have taken away the sanctity of communion and turned it into a party," a faithful church member complained as he left the church he had attended for more than thirty years.

"I don't understand our pastor," someone in a different church commented. "She says she is not liberal; but she surely ain't preaching the ol' time religion."

Another, halfway across the nation, writes, "I have been reading some of the books written by Christians in the Third World, and I find something strangely attractive in them, but I can't put my finger on it."

In a seminary, a student challenges a professor: "If you think Isaiah 53 refers to Israel, how could you read it in that Good Friday service as if it referred to Jesus?"

In a hospital, a doctor confides to the chaplain: "In Sunday school in my small southern town, they taught me one kind of religion. In college my favorite professor, as liberal as they come, taught me another. Now, as I must decide about machines, tubes, and plugs, neither is very helpful."

The common denominator in all these statements is perplexity. Christians are perplexed on at least two levels. First, they are perplexed by developments in Christian theology and liturgy which they cannot classify on the basis of the traditional polarities of liberal/fundamentalist or Catholic/Protestant. Second, and at a deeper level, they are perplexed by a world where new situations appear at an ever-accelerating speed, where "progress" offers hopes beyond our ancestors' wildest dreams and fears beyond their most dreadful nightmares.

The traditional theologies we have been taught, be they liberal or fundamentalist, do not offer much help in dealing with these perplexities. Indeed, some of them would lead us to believe that our perplexity itself is a lack of faith or a lack of understanding.

13

It is my contention that in the early church one finds, besides the distant ancestors of modern-day fundamentalisms and liberalisms, a third type of theology; that this third type leads to a different reading of the Bible and its message; and that this different reading is particularly relevant to our present-day perplexities. Therefore this essay is addressed primarily to Christians who, amidst the perplexities of the late twentieth century, are searching for an understanding of their faith that will lead them, with hope and obedience, into the twenty-first.

Almost thirty years ago when I began to teach the history of Christian thought, my main goal was to introduce my students to a history and a tradition which I considered both inspiring and significant for our contemporary understanding of the faith. Those lectures eventually took the shape of a book with the obvious title, *A History of Christian Thought*.[1]

The unimaginative character of that title was intentional. The purpose of the book was not to offer my own interpretation of the history of Christian theology, but simply to introduce readers to a standard interpretation of that history, as clearly and as faithfully as possible. Over the years, as that book has gone through some eleven printings and now a revised edition, I have rewritten portions in a number of ways. But I have sought to remain faithful to that original purpose, out of the conviction that students and other readers who are being introduced to the field, and who therefore may have difficulty distinguishing between scholarly consensus and my own interpretations, have the right to an introduction where such distinction is as clear as possible.

On the other hand, every history is an interpretation. I am fully aware that the "scholarly consensus" I have tried to expound is in itself a conglomerate of interpretations, that these have been guided not only by ancient documents and historical data, but by the historians' biases and agendas—often unknown to the historians themselves. Thus, as a historian, I cannot avoid interpretation. It is this that I propose to offer in the present work, which may be read either by itself or as an appendix to the earlier *History*.

That history is interpretation is not intended as a purely

negative statement, one reminding us of our intellectual finitude; it is also intended as a positive statement. This is precisely the difference between the historian and the antiquarian. The latter collects bits of information or antiques because they are interesting. The historian looks at the past from the present and at the present through the past. It is true that our present agendas leave an imprint on our interpretation of the past; but it is just as true that our reading of the past guides our present action. History is precisely that never-ending dialogue between past and present—both with a view to the future. It is in that dialogue that we are all engaged, whether we are professional historians or not. I invite the reader to join me in that dialogue as we revisit the salient points in the Christian tradition.

PART ONE

The Three Types in Their Classical Formulation

*T*OWARD the end of the second century and the beginning of the third, there were in the Christian church three major theological perspectives generally considered orthodox. These I shall call A, B, and C, following the order of our contemporary familiarity with them, not the chronological order of their appearance. While types A and B are best known to twentieth-century Western Christians, Type C is much older.

The difference between these three types of theology does not lie specifically in any one point of doctrine, but rather in their entire perspectives, which then are reflected in their understanding of every theological theme, from creation to the final consummation.

If it is true that Type C is the oldest of the three and that the other two remain within the bounds of what was considered orthodox at the time, one should not be surprised to find elements of Type C in the major exponents of types A and B. Therefore, this first thesis suggests that although one finds elements of one of these types in the others, there are perspectives and emphases that are characteristic of each of the three, and these provide for a theological outlook that is quite distinct.

Finally, these three types are not socially neutral. Each develops within social settings and agendas which, though perhaps unrecognized by its exponents, play an important role in its basic perspective.

I

Places and People

In reading the New Testament, one could well imagine that the center of theological activity for the Christian church during its early centuries was Jerusalem. On the other hand, looking at those early centuries from the perspective of later times, one might guess that the center of such activity was Rome, the capital city of the Empire. Both assumptions would be wrong.

Jerusalem, the birthplace of Christianity, was besieged and destroyed by the Romans in A.D. 70, in reprisal for a Jewish rebellion. A second revolt in A.D. 135 led the emperor to expel all Jews from Jerusalem and rebuild the city as a Roman town with the name Aelia Capitolina. As for Rome, there was a sizable Christian community in the city by the second century and that community produced a number of documents that have survived; but Rome was seldom the center of the intellectual life of the church.

The main centers of theological reflection and literary activity in the early centuries were Carthage, Alexandria, and an area in the northeastern Mediterranean which included both Syria—with its capital city Antioch—and Asia Minor.

Type A—Carthage, on the north coast of Africa near what is now the city of Tunis, was an ancient city founded around 800 B.C. by Phoenicians from Tyre. But in 146 B.C. the Romans conquered and destroyed it, following Cato's impassioned pleas to put an end to the apparently endless Punic wars by the annihilation of the enemy: *delenda est Carthago*—let Carthage be erased. Therefore, when the city was rebuilt as part of the Roman Empire at the beginning of the Christian era, it had all the appearance of a typically Roman town. Although the ruling classes in the city were of Roman, or at least of Italian extraction, below them was a large Latinized middle class whose members served as the instruments

19

of Roman administration. Even further below was the mass of the population, of ancient Berber stock, conquered first by the old Carthaginians and later by the Romans.[1]

The origins of Christianity in Carthage are not known. Although traditionally it has been thought that the new faith was brought from Rome, some scholars point to indications that it may have come directly from the East.[2] In any case, toward the end of the second century, a Christian community was already flourishing in Carthage. Of its bishop, Agrippinus, little is known except his name. But that church produced famous martyrs such as Perpetua and Felicitas.[3] It also produced Tertullian, the founder of Western Christian theology, who will serve as our main exponent for that understanding of the gospel which we call Type A theology.

Tertullian is probably the first Christian Latin writer whose works have survived.[4] He was born about the middle of the second century and converted to Christianity around A.D. 193. Soon he became one of the staunchest defenders of orthodoxy in the face of all sorts of heresy, although he himself eventually joined the sect of the Montanists. As will be seen later, that step is not altogether surprising in light of the main thrust of his theology.

At any rate, both while in the communion of the larger church and after becoming a Montanist, Tertullian was a prolific writer whose extant works are numerous. Through them he stamped his own seal on Western theology, while for the first time developing a Christian theological vocabulary in Latin. For these reasons he has been rightly considered the father of Latin theology. As such, he coined the terminology used to this day in Trinitarian and Christological formulas, as well as a number of such lapidary phrases as "The blood of Christians is seed" and "What indeed has Athens to do with Jerusalem? What concord is there between the Academy and the Church?"

It seems that Tertullian was a lawyer. In one of the sources by which ancient jurisprudence is known, there is mention of a certain "Tertullian" who may well have been our theologian. In any case, there is no doubt that his was a legal mind. In several of his writings one can discern the rhetorical structures which advocates at that time used to convince their hearers.[5] *On the*

Testimony of the Soul places the pagan soul on the witness stand and, through a process highly reminiscent of today's cross-examinations, forces that soul to confess that the Christian faith is eminently rational. In what would parallel a closing argument, Tertullian concludes: "Every soul is a culprit as well as a witness: in the measure that it testifies for truth, the guilt of error is in it."[6]

In another work, *Prescription Against Heretics,* Tertullian uses the legal argument then known as a "prescription" in order to deny the heretics any right to use Scripture in defense of their doctrines.[7] According to him, during all these past years the church has been using the Scriptures as its own, and therefore, by virtue of that right of long undisputed possession which Roman law calls *preascriptio,* the church owns the Scriptures. In consequence, any attempt on the part of heretics to use Scripture is a usurpation, and the church has no obligation to debate with heretics upon the meaning of Scripture.

Another case in which one can see the use Tertullian makes of legal arguments appears in his *Apology,* written in defense of Christianity. Here he tries to show the injustice of the laws enacted against Christians. At that time, the Roman Empire dealt with Christians generally in the same terms it had followed since the reign of Emperor Trajan early in the second century. According to Trajan's instructions to Governor Pliny of the province of Bithynia, the government should not employ its police resources in seeking out Christians; but if someone were accused of being a Christian, the authorities should investigate the matter, attempt to convince the accused to deny Christ and, if such persuasion did not succeed, apply the penalty of death. The reasons behind such a policy were complex, and this is not the place to discuss them. But Tertullian's words regarding such laws show his legal perspicacity:

> O miserable deliverance—under the necessities of the case, a self contradiction! It forbids them to be sought after as innocent, and it condemns them to be punished as guilty. It is at once merciful and cruel; it passes by, and it punishes. Why dost thou play a game of evasion upon thyself, O Judgment? It thou condemnest, why dost thou not also inquire? If thou dost not inquire, why dost thou not absolve?[8]

In his attitude toward pagan philosophy, Tertullian's position is curious. On the one hand, he claims that the origin of every heresy is to be found in philosophy, which heretics have mingled with the gospel. It is within this context that the famous words already quoted appear: "What indeed has Athens to do with Jerusalem? What concord is there between the Academy and the Church?"[9] But on the other hand, Tertullian approaches the gospel with a set of philosophical presuppositions drawn from Stoicism, which soon become clear to any astute reader of his works.

Stoicism was the prevalent philosophy in the western Roman Empire during the second century. Even Emperor Marcus Aurelius, who died in A.D. 180, was a follower of the way of the Stoics. This philosophy became popular in the Latin portion of the Empire, among other reasons, because its practical and ethical interest agreed with the practical penchant and legal traditions of Rome. Stoicism was, above all, a moral philosophy. To be wise was to live in harmony with the ruling order in all things, with natural law. Since most of those who were the pillars of Roman society believed that their society and its order were eminently rational, Stoicism was the philosophy that best suited their understanding of reality. As is so often the case, their understanding of "natural law" was essentially that which the most respected elements in their social class took to be so. For the Stoic, the final goal of wisdom is to discover the law of the universe and to live according to it. For such a one as Marcus Aurelius, being a wise Stoic philosopher was perfectly compatible with being a Roman ruler, for after all, the law of Rome was a concrete working out of universal natural law.

Breathing the pervasive atmosphere in which he lived, Tertullian viewed much of reality in the same fashion as did the Stoics. Furthermore, the Stoic emphasis on natural law was perfectly suited to his own legal penchant. Therefore, while decrying the intrusion of philosophy into theology, Tertullian himself, perhaps unaware, was a Stoic.[10]

In conclusion, if one were to seek a single word with which to characterize Tertullian's basic theological concern, that word would be *Law*. As he saw it, Christianity is superior to any human philosophy, since in it one receives the revelation of the ultimate law of the universe, the law of God.

In following this perspective, some forerunners of Tertullian in the Western church, while writing in Greek and not as absorbed in a legal mindset as he, did show some of the concerns that would come to the forefront in his writings. Even at the end of the first century, in Clement of Rome's *First Epistle to the Corinthians,* may be seen that Stoic influence which later would become so pervasive in Tertullian's theology.[11] By the middle of the second century, the legalistic tendencies in this approach to Christianity are evident in both the *Shepherd* of Hermas and the so-called *Second Epistle of Clement.* These two writings may be considered precursors of Tertullian, particularly in matters that had to do with the forgiveness of sins, to which we shall return in a later chapter. Together, all these writers exemplify the early development of Type A theology, as it took shape within the cradle of Roman practical and legal concerns.

Type B—Alexandria was destined to become the home of a very different type of theology—which we shall call Type B. While Carthage was the most Latin of the cities and areas to be discussed here, Alexandria was the most Hellenistic. As its name proclaims, Alexandria was founded by Alexander the Great, in 331 B.C. When Alexander's empire fell apart after his death, the great city he had founded in Egypt became the capital of the territories ruled by the Ptolemies, until the Romans captured it in 30 B.C.

Alexandria was at the mouth of the Nile, an enviable location for trade and transportation, and it soon became one of the most important cities in the entire Mediterranean basin. For the same reasons, it also became an intellectual center in which diverse philosophical and religious currents came together.

Alexandria was the home of the famous Museum, which was not a place for public exhibits of art or of ancient remains, as are our modern museums, but a center of service to the muses, similar to our modern-day universities, where scholars and scientists pursue all sorts of knowledge. Around the Museum, therefore, gathered people interested in such diverse studies as philosophy, astronomy, mathematics, zoology, and so on. The famous library of Alexandria, which served as a base for these studies, would compare favorably with many twentieth-century university libraries.

As was to be expected in such an environment, different religious doctrines and currents came together and mingled. The number of Jews in Alexandria and its surroundings was high and seems to have been so for a long time. Indeed, even in the seventh or sixth century B.C., long before the founding of the city, Jews were so numerous in upper Egypt, many miles up the Nile, that they had built a temple to their God. It was in Alexandria, in the last centuries before the birth of Jesus, that the Hebrew Bible was translated into Greek—the Septuagint. But the religious collage of that great city included also astrologers from Mesopotamia, Persian dualists, devotees of ancient Egyptian deities, and proponents of countless other doctrines and religious theories which often became so intermingled as to be hardly distinguishable from one another.

A letter attributed to Emperor Hadrian, addressed to his brother-in-law Servianus, describes the mood of Egypt, particularly of its main city, Alexandria:

> Dear Servianus, that Egypt which you so praised turns out to be flighty, vacillating, and always running after the latest fashion. There those who worship Serapis are Christians; and those who call themselves Christian bishops are devotees of Serapis. There is not a chief of the Jewish synagogue, nor a Christian elder, nor a Samaritan, who is not also a mathematician, a diviner, and a masseur for athletes.[12]

Granted, much of this is literary exaggeration. Still, it conveys the picture of a society where all sorts of science and wisdom mingled, often in rather uncritical ways.

The origins of Christianity in Alexandria, like those of Carthage, are unknown. Church historian Eusebius of Caesarea, writing in the fourth century, tells us that Saint Mark was in that city preaching the gospel.[13] But that piece of information, coming as it does from a time when the churches in various cities were seeking ways to claim apostolic origins, is hardly trustworthy. In any case, by the middle of the second century, a strong Christian community flourished in Alexandria. Toward the end of that century the community had within its fold such distinguished theologians as Origen, who will serve as our main exponent of Type B theology, and his forerunner Clement of Alexandria.

Clement was not a native of Alexandria, but of Athens. He left his native city in a quest for truth, which took him to various parts of the Empire and eventually to Alexandria. There he found what he sought: The Christian teacher Pantaenus introduced him to the "true philosophy" of Christianity. After some time Clement succeeded Pantaenus and taught until he was forced to leave the city during the persecution of Septimius Severus, early in the third century. He left behind his disciple Origen, destined to become the most famous teacher of the school of Alexandria. Although Clement, as we shall see, in many ways can be seen as an early exponent of Type B theology, in truth he stands between that and the much earlier Type C. It is therefore to Origen that we must turn primarily for our exposition of Type B.

Origen was a native of Alexandria, born in a Christian home around A.D. 185. In A.D. 202, when he was some seventeen years old, his father suffered martyrdom. The young lad wished to offer himself to the same fate, but his mother hid his clothes and thus prevented him from leaving the house. From a very early age, Origen began to teach the Scriptures, as well as what he called "the Christian philosophy"—first to new converts being prepared for baptism and eventually to more mature Christians. His fame grew to such a point that even the emperor's mother—a pagan—attended one of his lectures. In A.D. 231, due to tensions with the bishop of Alexandria, Origen left the city and moved to Caesarea, where he continued his studies and his teaching. He died in Tyre in A.D. 253 after undergoing torture because of his faith. During his lifetime, he wrote biblical commentaries, sermons, and other works at an incredible rate. It is said that on occasion he dictated seven different works simultaneously, to the same number of copyists.

As we have seen, the city of Alexandria, where Clement had

found a new home and Origen had spent his formative years, was an intellectual melting pot. Within that boiling intellectual activity, Origen came to occupy a distinguished place, and in the process he too suffered the influence of the currents that swirled around him. Therefore, in order to understand Origen's theology—and Clement's, to some extent—one must pause to describe that intellectual atmosphere.

Although the pervading mood of Alexandria was that of eclecticism, the prevalent philosophy was Platonic, concerned with discovering the immutable truth that lies behind the mutable realities perceived by the senses. Before Origen's time, that Platonic tradition had acquired certain elements from Stoicism, as well as from other sources, and thus became what historians of philosophy call middle Platonism.[14] During Origen's lifetime, this process continued even further, particularly by adding a religious dimension, thus giving birth to Neoplatonism.

For this entire tradition, the goal was to discover the immutable, purely rational truth that must exist beyond the reality the senses perceive. As a secondary trait, this new Platonism sought to adjust life to such eternal truth, and therefore included in it a moral element very similar to that of Stoicism.[15]

Such surroundings had influenced Alexandrine Judaism even before the advent of Christianity, as may be seen in the Greek translation of the Old Testament—the Septuagint—to which reference has been made. Such influence is much more marked in the thought of Philo of Alexandria, a Jewish contemporary of Jesus who understood the faith of his ancestors in terms of the Platonic tradition, and who sought to defend that faith against the criticism current in Alexandrian intellectual circles. It was said in those circles that the Jewish Scriptures simply told a series of stories with no philosophical value. In order to show that the Bible did indeed have philosophical significance, Philo interpreted it as a vast series of allegories, referring not so much to concrete historical facts as to eternal truths of a moral and metaphysical order. Thus the Hebrew Scriptures were made to coincide with Alexandrine philosophy, and Philo could affirm the value of both.

After Philo's time, the Platonic tradition gained an even stronger foothold in Alexandria.[16] Therefore when Origen appeared on the scene, that tradition was foremost in the intellectual circles of the city, to the point that Platonism, in its new modified forms, was taken to be tantamount to *philosophy*. The most famous teacher of this philosophy during Origen's youth was Ammonius Saccas, among whose disciples were Plotinus, the great proponent of mystical Neoplatonism, and probably Origen himself. The goal of philosophy from this entire perspective was to reach the ineffable, eternal, immutable One.

As part of that tradition, Origen also was seeking immutable truths, realities that would not be dependent upon sensory perception, and scriptural interpretations to show that the Bible sets forth a series of unalterable metaphysical and moral principles.

In short, if one were to summarize in a single word the central theme of Origen's thought, just as Tertullian's theology can best be understood in terms of *Law,* Origen's can best be characterized in terms of *Truth.*

Such truth, as Origen conceived of it, must be immutable and transcendent. It must be free of all the changes and vicissitudes of this world, which is subject to time and transition. Its knowledge does not come to us through sensory perception, but from two sources in agreement with each other: reason and revelation. Origen's forerunner Clement of Alexandria had said that all truth was one, and that therefore philosophy led essentially to the same truth, revealed in the Son.[17] Furthermore, philosophy was the handmaiden given by God to lead the Gentiles to Christ, just as God had given Scripture to the Jews for the same purpose.[18] Origen agreed with Clement in all this and therefore believed that his main task as a theologian was to discover and reveal the concordance between philosophy and the Christian faith.

While following this intellectual pursuit, Origen did not reject or feel contempt for the teaching of the church. On the contrary, he held firmly to it—and in later life suffered prison and torture. But for those points on which there was no clear teaching, he felt free, even compelled, to undertake speculations similar to those of the Alexandrian thinkers of his time. Of this, we shall see ample evidence later.

Type C—The third geographic center we shall consider is the **Northeastern Mediterranean,** an area roughly comprising Asia Minor and Syria—what is now Turkey, Syria, and the surrounding states.[19] The principal city in the northeast corner of the Mediterranean was Antioch.[20] Founded in 301 B.C. by Seleucus I, Nicator, who named it after his father Antiochus, Antioch became one of the most important cities in the Roman Empire. Since it was never razed by the Romans as were Jerusalem and Carthage, it retained a great deal of its ancient heritage and was much less Romanized than Carthage. Like Alexandria, Antioch was a meeting place for diverse religious and philosophical doctrines, although syncretism there does not appear to have reached the heights it attained in Alexandria. Particularly in the case of Judaism, the very large and ancient Jewish community in Antioch,[21] which kept in close contact with Jerusalem, was therefore less hellenized than its Alexandrian counterpart.

Thanks to the book of Acts, a great deal is known about the church in Antioch in the first century, although even there its origins are obscure and sometimes confused. Acts tells us that after Stephen's death the disciples, scattered by fear of persecution, took the gospel to Antioch. We are also told that those first disciples preached only to Jews but that some from Cyprus and Cyrene began preaching to Greeks, although the names of those early evangelizers, and their methods, are not known. In any case, it was at Antioch that the followers of the Way were first called Christians. It is also significant that the word *Christianity* first appears in the letters of a bishop of Antioch early in the second century.[22]

Many contacts between Antioch and Asia Minor are shown in the book of Acts. It is the church of Antioch that sends Paul and Barnabas on their missionary journeys, and these journeys take them to Asia Minor.

This region is known through several of Paul's epistles written to or from Asia Minor, the book of Revelation, and probably several other books of the new Testament. Many scholars ascribe the Gospel of Matthew to Antioch, and the Gospel and epistles of John are traditionally associated with Ephesus. Indeed, the connection between this corner of the Mediterranean basin and the greater part of the New Testament is such that a knowledge of the theology that flourished there in the second century will provide significant insight into the meaning of the New Testament itself.

The Christianity of this region is known also through a number of other witnesses. Foremost among these is Bishop Ignatius of Antioch, who early in the second century was being taken as a prisoner to Rome, where he was to suffer martyrdom. On his way, within the brief compass of two weeks, Ignatius wrote seven letters which have been preserved. Some time later his younger friend Polycarp, bishop of Smyrna, wrote to the Philippians inquiring about Ignatius. Polycarp's letter, which some scholars believe to have been two,[23] also has been preserved. In the middle of the second century Polycarp himself was martyred, and the account of his martyrdom, perhaps written in part by an eyewitness, reflects the theology prevalent in the region.

At approximately the same time, Papias, bishop of Hierapolis, also in Asia Minor, was compiling "Sayings of the Lord," which were not included in the Gospels. Only brief quotations of his works have survived, but these show theological points of contact with other writings from that area. In Antioch around the year A.D. 180, Bishop Theophilus wrote his *Three Books to Autolycus*, which also reflect the theology of the region. Somewhat earlier, Justin Martyr composed his two apologies and *Dialogue with Trypho*. Although in many ways his works exhibit the theological tradition of Antioch and Asia Minor (Justin was a native of Samaria), in other ways he is a forerunner of what would appear later in Alexandria with Clement and Origen. Therefore he may be said to stand somewhere between our Type B and Type C.

The most significant exponent of the theology of the northeastern Mediterranean, however, was Irenaeus, who spent most of his life in Lyon. He will be our main exponent of Type C theology, although on occasion we shall point out that similar views are found in some of his predecessors.[24]

We do not know why Irenaeus had moved to Lyon, hundreds of miles away from his native Smyrna. He was part of a community of believers there, many of whom also seem to have migrated from Asia Minor, or at least from other parts of the Greek-speaking world.[25] In any case, the tradition Irenaeus carried with him to Gaul reflected what was current in Asia Minor. His theological ancestors, besides Polycarp, are the book of Revelation, which includes a letter addressed to the church in Smyrna; the Fourth Gospel, from which he draws constantly; and other such kindred minds as Ignatius of Antioch, Theophilus, and—to a degree—Justin Martyr.

As we compare Irenaeus with Tertullian and Origen, the contrast is clear. In the first place, of the three, only Irenaeus was actually the shepherd of a congregation. If he decided to spell out his theological views, it was because certain doctrines he considered false were threatening the well-being of his flock, or because that flock needed a clear and concise introduction to the Christian faith. Second, he was not a prolific writer, as were Tertullian and Origen. He has left behind only two major works and a few fragments quoted by later authors.

Finally, Irenaeus boasted closer links with the subapostolic tradition than did the other two. In Smyrna, where he spent his early years, he was a disciple of Polycarp, who in turn was a disciple of "John" in Ephesus. While it is not clear exactly who this "John" was, there is no doubt that the early church—particularly in Asia Minor—regarded him either as one of the Twelve, or as someone having very direct connection with them. Irenaeus apparently believed that "John" was John the Apostle, with whom he had a direct link through his own teacher Polycarp. The historian Eusebius quotes one of Irenaeus' lost writings:

> I remember the events of that time more clearly than those of recent years. For what boys learn, growing with their mind, becomes joined with it; so that I am able to describe the very place in which the blessed Polycarp sat as he discoursed, and his goings

out and his comings in, and the manner of his life, and his physical appearance, and his discourses to the people, and the accounts which he gave of his intercourse with John and with the others who had seen the Lord. And as he remembered these words, and what he heard from them concerning the Lord, and concerning his miracles and his teachings, having received from the eyewitnesses of the "Word of life," Polycarp related all things in harmony with the Scriptures. These things being told me by the mercy of God, I listened to them attentively, noting them down, not on paper, but in my heart. And continually, through God's grace, I recall them faithfully.[26]

Since Palestine, Antioch, and Asia Minor were lands where many of the events related in the New Testament took place, Christians there had deeper rootage in the history of the Christian faith than did those in Alexandria or Carthage. For them, the essence of the faith was not to be found in a series of immutable truths which had come down from heaven, but in certain events which had taken place right there, among those from whom they had received their faith. Even centuries after the time of Irenaeus, this could be seen in the theological tradition historians call "the school of Antioch," particularly in matters that had to do with Christology.[27]

From all this we see that Irenaeus' theology was eminently pastoral. He himself was a pastor, and his writings had pastoral purposes. But even further, Irenaeus saw God as the great Shepherd who leads the flock toward the divine purposes. So just as it is possible to characterize Tertullian's main thrust as *Law* and Origen's as *Truth*, one can say that Irenaeus' central theme is *History*. It is not, however, history in the sense of a faithful narrative of past events—although such events are indeed part of history—but rather in the sense that all that takes place within time is guided toward God's future.[28] At creation, God had certain goals which were to be fulfilled through the process of history. In spite of sin, those goals have not been abandoned, and right now God, the great Shepherd, still continues to lead history toward them.

Thus, toward the end of the second century and the beginning of the third there were in the Christian church three main currents of theological thought. Type A's main proponent was Tertullian at Carthage, whereas B had its center in Alexandria, where its main exponent was Origen. Type C, which had roots in the much older theology of Antioch and Asia Minor, is best seen in the writings of Irenaeus. In the next chapters we shall try to show more clearly how each of these three perspectives views the central themes of Christian theology. Before continuing, it may be helpful to summarize in the following chart what has been said:

The Three Types

	A	B	C
Three Areas	Carthage	Alexandria	Asia Minor and Syria
Three Theologians	Tertullian	Origen	Irenaeus
Main Interest	Moral	Metaphysical	Pastoral
Main Category	Law	Truth	History
Philosophical Orientation	Stoic	Platonic	None in particular
Forerunners	Clement of Rome Hermas Second Clement	Philo (Justin) Clement of Alexandria	Much of NT Ignatius Polycarp Theophilus

At this point, a word of warning is in order. Any typology is of necessity schematic. It may be illuminating, as long as it is not taken too literally. In this respect, a typology is like a caricature: When one sees a caricature of a person, one immediately recognizes the person by the exaggeration of prominent features, although no one could possibly have such features. Likewise, in drawing a typology such as that being presented here, one underscores those elements most characteristic of a particular type. This helps clarify the issues and contrasts, as long as it is not understood as an actual description that makes all nuances superfluous. Indeed, if it is true that Type C theology is much older than the other two, one should not be surprised to find elements of it in Tertullian or Origen. And since types A and B were considered orthodox, one will find their influence among theologians we would generally classify as exponents of Type C.

In the pages that follow, I shall attempt to remind the reader of this schematic nature of typologies by listing in the footnotes some examples of cases in which an exponent of a particular type includes elements which I have said are characteristic of another type. In spite of this, however, I believe the typology still holds and is helpful for understanding both the course of the history of Christian thought and some of the challenges Christian theology faces today.

II

God, Creation, and Original Sin

At the time of the theologians whose work we are studying, the church faced the challenge of paganism—and its concrete political form, persecution—in addition to the inner challenge of heresies. It is within these two contexts that the theology of Irenaeus, Tertullian, and Origen is to be understood.

Paganism was a challenge to the church, above all, because it was supported by political power and social custom. If the pagan gods were true gods and the Christian deity false, Christians were no more than social deviants, which would seem to justify their persecution. Theologically, Christians also were well aware that pagan polytheism was radically incompatible with their own monotheism.[1] Pagans had a different god for each sphere of human life—Mars for war, Venus for love, and so on. On occasion these gods could oppose one another, and human beings and even nations could be the pawns in their battles. Over against this, Christians, jointly with Jews, insisted that there is only one God, who rules the universe and every sphere of life.

It was in response to the challenge of paganism—in particular, its polytheistic faith—that some of the earliest Christian theological treatises were written—by Justin, Tatian, Athenagoras, et al. The principal aim of the works of two of the theologians we are studying, Tertullian and Origen, was to refute the pagans' accusations against Christians. Therefore a great deal of what these theologians have to say regarding Christian monotheism and the doctrine of creation should be understood within the context of their polemic against polytheism.

"Heresies" were the main danger our authors had to face, a danger greater than paganism. Several doctrines appeared within the church, which, in the opinion of the majority, endangered the very core of the faith. This did not mean that the church wished all to think exactly alike. On the contrary, as we shall see, several theological currents existed within the church, and all were equally permitted. But also, certain other opinions seemed to deny essential aspects of the faith such as monotheism, creation, and the incarnation of God in Jesus Christ. These latter opinions were soon rejected by the church at large and given the name *heresies*.

The most important of these heresies was gnosticism. The name derives from its adherents' belief that salvation is obtained through secret *knowledge* or *gnosis*. To this day, scholars are not agreed as to the origin of gnosticism. It seems to have sprung from diverse roots in Babylonian astrology, Greek philosophy, mystery religions, Jewish apocalypticism, and other sources.[2] Converts to Christianity from various backgrounds brought these doctrines into the church, where gnosticism soon became a very real threat.

What interests us here, however, is not the question of the origins of gnosticism, but its main tenets and why the great teachers of the church opposed it. At first sight, gnosticism seemed diametrically opposed to polytheism, for most Gnostic systems began by postulating the existence of a single source for all reality. This first principle, which some called Abyss, existed eternally, and from it sprang other spiritual beings which the Gnostics called eons.[3] The purpose of the eons was to glorify the Abyss. But one eon, either by error or intentionally, gave birth to this material world.

The consequence of this mythology is that gnosticism, which begins by affirming a single principle of all being, ends by asserting a radical dualism with reference to actual existence. Spiritual reality, which either still resides in the eons or proceeds from them, is good, whereas material reality, coming as it does from the error of an eon, is evil. The physical world is not the result of a decision on the part of the Supreme Being, but rather of an error.

This in turn means that the human being, composed of a material and a spiritual reality, finds within itself the same dualism that exists in the outer world. The body is evil and is necessarily destined to destruction, whereas the spirit, which belongs to the sphere of the eons, will inevitably return to it. When Gnostics applied these ideas to the Christian message, many reached the conclusion that Christ had not really come in the flesh, since flesh was evil, but had been a purely spiritual being, with flesh that was either a mere appearance or a heavenly, spiritual substance.[4] Likewise, Gnostics felt compelled to deny the resurrection of the body and be content with the immortality of the soul.[5]

This meant that gnosticism, like pagan polytheism, divided the universe into various "spheres of influence." While polytheists assigned a different sphere of activity to each god, Gnostics achieved a similar result by claiming that the material world was alien to the Supreme Being.

The case of Marcion was somewhat different;[6] although he approached gnosticism at many points, in others he differed radically. Marcion did not believe in a long series of "eons." He held, rather, that the God Jehovah of the Old Testament was not the same as the Father who sent Jesus to the world. Jehovah was an inferior god who made this world either out of ignorance, or out of spite against the Supreme God, and placed us in it. Above Jehovah is the loving Father of Jesus. Jehovah is vindictive and demands justice, while the Father is loving and forgiving. *Law* is Jehovah's theme; *grace* is the Father's. The Old Testament, the Jewish Bible, is without any doubt the word of a god—but not of the Supreme God. It is the word of that lesser being called Jehovah. Over against the religion of the Old Testament, the Christian message is one of pure love and pardon. The Christian God does not punish. The Christian God never would have made this world, with its strife and suffering. But the Father did have mercy upon us, imprisoned as we are in this world where we had been placed by Jehovah, and therefore the Father sent Jesus to save us.

Since Marcion believed that this world was the creation of Jehovah and that its matter was subject to the power of that lesser god, it followed that Jesus did not come into the world through the natural way of human birth, for this would have placed him under the lordship of Jehovah. Therefore, Marcion declared that during the reign of Tiberius, Jesus appeared in the world as a mature man, but his flesh was not like ours.

Such views, as well as the challenges of paganism, were the background against which our three theologians developed their understanding of God, creation, and original sin.

Type A—Although **Tertullian** wrote several works against the various heresies of his time, it was against Marcion that he wrote his most extensive, and therefore a great deal of his doctrine of God and creation was directed against Marcionite teachings. This is not surprising, for Marcion's insistence on grace to the point of obliterating the role of law in the Christian gospel must have been quite disturbing to Tertullian's legalistic mind.

As one studies what Tertullian has to say, one discovers once again his legal and juridical interest. For him, God is above all a legislator and a judge. Naturally, part of this emphasis is due to the attempt to refute Marcion, who claimed that only the God of the *Old* Testament judges and punishes. But it is also due to Tertullian's fundamental perspective.

In Stoicism, a doctrine the imprint of which can be found repeatedly in Tertullian's works, the universe is an ordered system. It is worthy of the name *universe* precisely because of the laws which govern the course of all that exists within it. From such a perspective, if there is a Supreme Being, that being must above all be a legislator—a principle of order which establishes the law of nature by which all must abide.

Tertullian then combines Stoic teachings with what the Bible says about the law of God and depicts God primarily as ruler and legislator. Some fifty years earlier, another Western writer, Clement of Rome, whose theological orientation was in some points similar to that of Tertullian, had called God "the despot" of the universe.[7] By this he did not mean that God was a tyrant, but rather that God ruled over all things; at that time the word *despot* did not have the meaning it now has, but meant simply "sovereign king." Now Tertullian followed a similar line of thought, telling Marcion that "nothing is so unworthy of the Divine Being as not to execute retribution on what He has disliked or forbidden."[8] God has given laws and established an order, and anyone who disobeys those laws or strays from that order ought to expect divine retribution: "For how is it possible that he should issue commands, if he does not mean to execute them; or forbid sins, if he intends not to punish them, but rather to decline the functions of the judge, as being a stranger to all notions of severity and judicial chastisement?"[9]

The same may be seen in the way Tertullian discusses the doctrine of the Trinity. To him belongs the honor of first having employed the formula that later became classic—"one substance and three persons." However, most revealing for our purposes is the way he explains this formula. At that time, both *person* and *substance* were terms used in legal circles. The first was used in a manner similar to our own when we speak of a "legal person." The second referred to the possessions or position of a person, which determined that person's place in society—as today we speak of someone as "a person of substance." Applying that terminology, Tertullian says that, just as the emperor may share his empire with his son without thereby dividing it, so can the Father share divinity with the Son and the Holy Spirit without thereby dividing that divinity. Hence the famous formula "one substance and three persons." The most significant point in all this, from the point of view of our interest here, is that once again Tertullian has made use of forensic ideas—in this case to develop his doctrine of the Trinity—and has once again compared God with an earthly sovereign or legislator.[10]

Tertullian's understanding of creation takes shape vis-à-vis Marcion's denial. Over against this, Tertullian states that all that exists has been created by God. The flesh is a creature of God as much as the soul, and Scripture on occasion decries the flesh only because the soul uses it to carry out its evil intentions. In a typically sarcastic passage, Tertullian affirms that his God has created the entire world; then he challenges Marcion to produce at least "a stray vegetable" created by *his* God.[11] Also, in a separate polemic against Hermogenes, who believed the world was made of a preexistent matter, Tertullian asserted the doctrine of creation out of nothing, which eventually became standard Christian doctrine.[12]

However, what most interests us here is the manner in which Tertullian conceives the original creation. Since God's universe was strictly ordered, that original creation was God's final intent.[13] In general, Tertullian's theology does not look to the future except as a return to the original order of creation, now transmuted to the heavenly mansions. In other words, since the original state was a perfect order, it was God's final purpose, and all that has happened since is due to sin.[14] This static way of seeing the relationship between creation and God's ultimate goals—which due to our tradition appears to us the most common—tends to imply that all history is the result of sin; that God's original purpose did not include the existence of history. As will be seen later, Type A theology coincides with Type B on this point, and it was Augustine who made this perspective—or one very similar to it—normative in the West.

Another point at which Tertullian has had great importance for the history of Christian thought—and in particular for what, from the perspective of our tradition, appears as normative Christian doctrine—is his view of original sin. For most of us, the phrase "original sin" evokes the image of something we have supposedly inherited from our ancestors—in the last analysis, from Adam and Eve. It was thus that Tertullian understood it, in marked contrast to both Origen and Irenaeus, whose views on the matter we shall examine later in this chapter. For Tertullian, original sin was an inheritance. Due to his Stoic tendencies, he had no difficulty conceiving the soul in materialistic terms, as an extremely subtle sort of body. He therefore believed that just as we inherit the characteristics of our bodies, we inherit those of our souls. Among those inherited traits is sin, and it is for this reason that we are all born sinners.[15]

These three elements—God as judge and legislator; creation as a perfect and finished order; and original sin as something we inherit—are Tertullian's contributions to the subjects under discussion in the present chapter. Their impact on the history of Western Christian thought has been such that to this day some of us take for granted that this is the only way orthodox Christianity can approach these subjects. However, as we study our two other types of theology we shall discover that there are other perspectives, particularly in Type C, which may be much more helpful in our efforts to understand the message of the Bible and bring it to bear on our present situation.

Type B—Turning now to **Origen,** we find that, while also opposing both pagan polytheism and Gnostic teaching, he understands God, creation, and original sin very differently from Tertullian. Origen's views show the impact of Plato and other thinkers of that philosophical tradition.

Half a century before Origen's time, in their effort to refute the criticisms of cultured pagans against Christianity, Justin and others had found a valuable ally in Platonism. To objections that the Christian God could not be seen, unlike those to be found on display in all the temples of the Empire, Christians could respond that the wisest among pagan thinkers had known that there was a Supreme Being from which all other beings derived. Plato had spoken of a Supreme Idea of Good or of Beauty, the source of all. Now Christians found it convenient to appropriate these words and claim that the God of Scripture, the Father of Jesus Christ, was that Supreme Being of which the philosophers had spoken.

Soon that argument became normative for the way in which Christians themselves understood their faith. Thus Clement of Alexandria, Origen's great forerunner, turned Platonism into one of his main instruments for understanding Scripture. In consequence, both Clement and Origen came to the conclusion that all Scripture concerning God must be understood in such a manner that it is compatible with what the philosophers had said about the Supreme Being.

It is for this reason that Type B theology tends to speak of God as the Ineffable One and to underscore the distance between the Godhead and the material world. God is absolutely transcendent, far beyond anything our intellect can conceive.[16] Our words can neither describe God nor approximate such a description, and therefore the only proper way to speak of the Godhead is to say what God is not: God is not mortal, not finite, not limited in any way, not subject to change. Or, in more traditional theological jargon, God is immortal, infinite, unlimited, impassible, and so on.

Starting from this idea, Origen claims that Scripture is always to be interpreted so that it does not contradict the supreme majesty of God. Thus, for instance, when the Bible speaks of the hands, heart, eyes, and such of God, this is not to be understood literally. The same is to be said of feelings like love, hate, or wrath.[17] Such things are "unworthy of God." Obviously, this often requires an allegorical interpretation of Scripture, to which we shall return later.

The main logical difficulty with such an understanding is that it makes it impossible to account for a relationship between God and the world.[18] At this point, one is reminded of the difficulty Plato always had in explaining how his eternal ideas related to the particular and the historical—a difficulty with which he struggled unsuccessfully in the *Parmenides*.

Half a century before Origen's time, the problem of the relationship between the immutable God and the mutable world was faced by Justin—and even earlier, among Platonizing Jews, by Philo. If God is transcendent and immutable, the question must then be faced: How can such a God relate to a mutable world? Justin's solution, which took its cue from other pagan and Jewish thinkers, was to make the Logos, or Word, an intermediary between God and the world.

Much later, a similar understanding would be one of the pillars of the more philosophically inclined among the Arians. But, as Athanasius would perspicaciously point out to his Arian opponents, this does not solve the problem. On the contrary, it compounds it, for one must then ask whether the Logos is mutable or immutable. If mutable, there is no difficulty in communication between the world and the Logos. But how can a mutable Logos communicate with an immutable God or reveal that God to the world? On the other hand, if immutable, such a Logos would have no difficulty relating to God, whose true revelation it could be, but it would not be able to relate to the mutable world.[19] Justin's very unphilosophical solution, which soon was rejected because it bordered on polytheism, was to speak of the Logos as a "second God," claiming that it somehow is less divine than the immutable God.[20]

In any case, the main point here is that for Type B theology, God is first of all the absolutely transcendent Ineffable One, "a simple intellectual nature," of which one can predicate love, wrath, and so on, only in a figurative manner.

Origen's doctrine of creation is much more interesting, although it never has been generally accepted by Christian theology, even within Type B. Origen was a biblical scholar, well aware—as others had been before him—that two different creation narratives are present in Genesis. Present-day scholars explain those narratives as originating from two distinct sources, brought together into a single text. Origen's solution, though not entirely original,[21] was that the Bible includes two different creations.[22]

In the first, God made only spirits, with the intention that the entire creation would remain spiritual. In the first creation, Genesis says that God made the human being after the divine image, and "male and female." According to Origen, this means that there was no distinction of sexes simply because there were no bodies; God had created intellects, whose purpose was to contemplate and commune with the One. And had there been no sin, this would have been the end of creation.

But sin intervened. Some spirits strayed from the contemplation of the One, for which they had been created, and the result was their fall. This would have led them to the abyss of nonexistence, had it not been for God's mercy, which gave them a temporary abode where they could reside until they were ready to return to their original purity. That temporary abode is the material creation, the world as we now know it, to which the second story of Genesis refers. Here the spirits of the original creation (now called souls) received bodies, and it is for this reason that in this narrative, God created man first and then woman. Sex, as all other bodily characteristics and functions, is part of this second creation, where we are to reside until we are ready to return to the heavenly realm for which we were originally intended.

It goes without saying that this notion of two creations was not favorably received within the church. Among other things, it implied the preexistence of souls, a pagan doctrine which Christians soon rejected.

However, what interests us here is not so much the content of Origen's doctrine of creation as the reasons that led him to it. For him, as for his entire philosophical tradition, intellectual life was superior to bodily life. The intellect, or the spirit—which for Origen was the same—was so far superior to matter that he could not conceive that the latter could be part of God's ultimate plan and was thus forced to posit a double creation. The second creation, which includes matter, was not part of God's original plan. Notice how this approaches gnosticism and Marcionism, in the claim that the present world is not the creation of God, but of a lesser being. Origen rejects that Gnostic doctrine, but in the end says that, although God indeed made this world, its creation was the result of the creatures' sin, not the eternal will of the Creator.

This in turn implies that for Origen, history is the result of sin, not only in the sense that the actual course of history is tainted by sin, but also in the deeper sense that the very existence of a world in which time runs is due to sin. Once again, Origen believes that truth must be timeless.[23] It could then be said that history is an interloper in the divine plan, which included only the existence of a spiritual and timeless creation.

Following the same line of thought when discussing God's image in the human creature, Origen insists that this does not refer in any way to the body, but to the spiritual and intellectual nature of the human being, which is "incorporeal, invisible, incorruptible, and immortal." Furthermore, the "vanity" to which the world is subject according to Romans is "nothing else than the body."[24]

Origen's doctrine of original sin also follows from all this: Every human being is a sinner at the moment of birth. But this is not due, as Tertullian would have said, to our inheritance from Adam and Eve, but to the fact that we sinned in our previous existence, when we were pure intellects. And it is precisely as a result of that sin that we find ourselves in the present world.

This understanding of original sin, which Origen takes almost directly from Plato and his understanding of the reason for the presence of souls in this world, was never accepted by the church at large, although in various times and places it has been resurrected by groups with theosophic tendencies. In general, later exponents of Type B theology have abandoned Origen on this point to follow his forerunner Clement of Alexandria. To Clement, original sin and the story of the fall in Eden were symbols which serve to indicate that all people sin on their own account, and sin is therefore both personal and universal.[25]

Type C—In agreement with our two other theologians, **Irenaeus** underscores God's unicity and power. Like Origen, he believes that God is eternal. But unlike the Alexandrine theologian, he does not shy away from other attributes that would seem to be more anthropomorphic:

> He is a simple, uncompounded Being, without diverse members, and altogether like, and equal to Himself, since He is wholly understanding, and wholly spirit, and wholly thought, and wholly intelligence, and wholly reason, and wholly hearing, and wholly seeing, and wholly light, and the whole source of all that is good.[26]

Note that in this passage, the language of which seems very philosophical, Irenaeus attributes to God not only intellect and spirit, but also sight and hearing. Irenaeus' main concern is not the avoidance of anthropomorphic language, but the attainment of an accurate description of the God of Scripture and of Christian worship and piety. For Christians, God is above all a Father, who in these latter days has adopted them as children. According to Irenaeus, this is what sets Christians apart from Gentiles, for whom God is "maker, creator, and almighty," and from Jews, for whom God is "lord and legislator." This does not mean that the Christian God does not have such characteristics, but rather that the gospel teaches that the God the philosophers worshiped only as the omnipotent creator, and the Jews only as sovereign lawgiver, is also and above all Father.[27] There is no doubt that in describing the Jewish God in this manner, Irenaeus is misrepresenting the faith of Israel, for in the Old Testament, God is much more than a monarch and a lawgiver. Unfortunately, such misrepresentation is to be found in all three of our theologians, as well as in much Christian theology since that time.

Irenaeus' doctrine of the Trinity merits special attention. We have already referred to Tertullian's formula, "one substance and three persons," which had the good fortune to become universally acknowledged, although with a somewhat different meaning than its creator attached to it. And in the case of Origen and the tradition of which he was part, we have discussed the manner in which they used the doctrine of the Logos, or Word, as a bridge between the immutable One and the mutable world. Irenaeus does not try to ascend to the philosophical heights of Origen, nor does he offer brilliant formulas as Tertullian does. For him, the question of how the three persons of the Trinity relate to one another is quite secondary. What is important is to know that God is Father, Son, and Holy Ghost, and to realize what this means for the way God relates to the world and to us.

The image Irenaeus most characteristically uses to refer to the Son and the Holy Spirit is "the hands of God." This image, which many interpreters of Irenaeus have found objectionable because it seemed exceedingly anthropomorphic, merits our attention. Of course, Irenaeus does not mean that God literally has two hands and that these are to be called the Word (or Son) and the Holy Spirit. His purpose in using this image is rather to show that God does relate directly with the world. While Justin, Clement, Origen, and the entire tradition which springs from them tend to separate God from the world, using the second person of the Trinity—the Word, Logos, or Son—as a link between the two, Irenaeus speaks of a God whose very hands enter into the world in the work of creation and in the leading of history. The Word and the Holy Spirit are not means to safeguard the distance between God and the world, but exactly the opposite—they serve to avoid any such distance.[28]

Turning now to the doctrine of creation, we find once again that Irenaeus' interests are not primarily speculative, but practical and pastoral. It is useless to know all the mysteries of creation if such knowledge does not lead to the love of God. "It is therefore better . . . that one should have no knowledge whatever of any one reason why a single thing in creation has been made, but should believe in God, and continue in His love, than that, puffed up through knowledge of this kind, he should fall away from that love which is the life of man."[29]

Thus Irenaeus' doctrine of creation does not evince the speculative tones of Origen's doctrine. What interests Irenaeus—and here he agrees with Tertullian—is not how or why God made the world, but the basic fact that the entire world is created by God.

On the other hand, while Tertullian uses the doctrine of creation to show that it is God who established the laws that rule the universe and that therefore we are to obey those laws, Irenaeus, without denying that point, sees much more in the doctrine of creation. For him, creation was not the end, but the beginning of God's relations with human creatures. Since history is the fundamental category of Irenaeus' thought, he sees in creation the very beginning of history, which is not then the result of sin. Even had there been no sin, there would have been history, although, naturally, it would have taken a different course.

It is for this reason that Irenaeus refers to the Genesis narrative as "the beginning of creation."[30] What God made at that time was only the beginning, which was expected to develop later through a historical process.

Irenaeus expresses this by affirming that Adam and Eve were created "like children."[31] This is not his own invention, but is found earlier in the writings of Theophilus of Antioch,[32] in those of Clement of Alexandria,[33] and was fairly common in Eastern Christianity for several centuries.[34] In the case of Irenaeus—and several other early theologians—the original perfection of creation is not to be understood in the sense that it was absolutely finished, with no room left for growth and development. On the contrary, God's purpose was that the human creature would grow in such a way as to enable it to enjoy an ever increasing fellowship with the divine.

It is within this context that the "image of God" or *imago Dei* is to be understood. According to Colossians 1:15, the image of God is none other than Jesus Christ. Therefore, being made "after the image of God" means that humankind has been created with Jesus Christ as a model. God did not make human beings and then decide to take human form in the incarnation, but rather, from the very beginning, God meant to become incarnate, and therefore used the incarnate Word as a model for Adam and Eve.[35]

This obviously implies that the incarnation was part of God's original plan and not due only to sin. We shall return to this subject, but here it will suffice to point out that, no matter how strange it may seem to modern Western Christians, this was a fairly common theme in early Christian theology—and well into the Middle Ages.[36]

In consequence, human beings were created good—not in the sense that they were finished, but in the sense that they were made from the model of the incarnate Word. They had the capacity to grow to further resemble that Word and therefore would come to the point of being able to enjoy close communion with the Creator.[37] Eventually, humans were to become higher than the angels.

Angels were like a prince's tutors.[38] Although tutors have temporary authority over the prince, they know that eventually they will have to surrender that authority and be placed under their former disciple. Angels are the mentors of human beings, who are called to be adoptive children of God and heirs of the divine power and glory.[39]

Viewed from this perspective, sin is understood very differently than from the viewpoints of either Type A or Type B. Sin does not consist in breaking a somewhat arbitrary law imposed by the Creator, nor in ceasing to contemplate the divine. Since God is above all a shepherd and a parent, the purpose of divine laws is to guide us in our own development. A shepherd does not lead the flock along a certain path for the sole purpose of showing power and authority. A human parent does not establish rules of conduct for the sheer pleasure of being obeyed, but from the conviction that those rules will benefit the children. Likewise, the laws established by God serve the human creature in its own process of growth and development toward closer communion with God.

The Creator placed man and woman in the garden so that they could grow in wisdom, thus becoming ever closer to their wise Creator, preparing for the time when they would be ready to learn justice. The laws which ruled life in Paradise were not intended to glorify God, as if the Creator were a pedant whose superiority must be shown at every turn. Their function was rather to train Adam and Eve in the knowledge of God.[40] The prohibition against eating the fruit of the tree was not intended to be permanent. On the contrary, God intended that humans would eventually acquire the knowledge of good and evil, live eternally, and be "like gods."[41]

But through the Serpent's prompting, Adam and Eve tried to short-circuit God's plans. Just as the small tot who tries to run may fall and be hurt, Adam and Eve, upon eating of the forbidden fruit, had anticipated the divine order.

But even in the midst of sin, God does not cease loving humanity. Though death may seem a curse, it is not really such, for it frees us from a life eternally subject to sin.[42] God decrees death, knowing that eventually through Jesus Christ, those who have died will live again, now in closer communion with their Creator.[43] After expelling them from the garden, God still showed love and mercy toward Adam and Eve by providing them with furs with which to clothe themselves.[44]

The result of sin was that humankind became subject to Satan.[45] In refusing to obey God, Adam and Eve became servants of the Serpent. And since they were the entirety of human-kind—or as Irenaeus would say, the "head" of humanity—in them we all were made subject to that evil power. Original sin, then, does not consist merely in an inheritance from our ancestors, as Tertullian and, in general, Type A theology would say, nor is it a way of speaking of our individual actions, as with Type B theology, but is rather the consequence of human solidarity when it is turned to evil. Literally, then, "in Adam we all have sinned."

This may be one of the most difficult elements in the theology of Irenaeus—and probably also in the New Testament—for the modern mind to grasp. We are used to thinking in individualistic terms, while Irenaeus believed that all humankind was like a single body, whose head was Adam. When Adam, the head, sinned, the entire body—that is, we—sinned with him. A modern illustration would be the case of those who are born Americans because their ancestors immigrated to these lands. In a sense, they came with their ancestors, whose migration determined their citizenship and, to an extent, even the legal and political system under which they would live. Had there been only one original immigrant couple, one could say that all the rest came to this land in them—that all their descendants are one body, with that original couple as the head. Later we shall see, in Irenaeus' doctrine of redemption, the crucial importance of this emphasis on human solidarity and our common bondage to sin.

However, before we continue our exposition and comparison of the three types of early theology, it may be well to incorporate some new elements into our chart:

The Three Types

	A	B	C
Three Areas	Carthage	Alexandria	Asia Minor and Syria
Three Theologians	Tertullian	Origen	Irenaeus
Main Interest	Moral	Metaphysical	Pastoral
Main Category	Law	Truth	History
Philosophical Orientation	Stoic	Platonic	None in particular
Forerunners	Clement of Rome Hermas Second Clement	Philo (Justin) Clement of Alexandria	Ignatius Polycarp Theophilus
God	Lawgiver Judge	Ineffable One Transcendent	Shepherd Father
Creation	Complete	Originally spiritual Double	Begun
Sin	Breaking the Law	Not contemplating the One	Anticipatory disobedience
Original Sin	Inherited	Individual	One sinned for all (human solidarity)

III

The Way of Salvation

It follows from the foregoing that each of our three theologians will see the way of salvation and its goal in a different way. Tertullian, Origen, and Irenaeus agree with the rest of the church that human beings stand in need of salvation. It is when one seeks further clarification that the different emphases of our three theologians begin to emerge.

Type A—Tertullian believes that we have broken God's law, and we therefore deserve to be punished. In other words, for him the human problem is, above all, a legal debt. Just as we say that a criminal "owes a debt to society," the sinner owes a debt to God. Our problem is then that we must find the means to cover that debt—or, in theological language, to offer satisfaction to God.[1]

Since we are debtors, our way to salvation is to pay that debt by repenting for our sins. Here Tertullian points out, as was to be expected within the framework of his theological perspective, that the reason we are to repent is not that repentance is good (although in fact it *is*), but that God has commanded it.[2] God has set a price for the forgiveness of our sins, and that price is repentance. This must be sincere repentance, for otherwise it would be like repaying God with counterfeit money—and the Lord, like a wise merchant, tests the coin before accepting it.[3]

Within all this, the role of Jesus Christ is not altogether clear in Tertullian's theology. There is no doubt that he is the Savior and that without him no one can be saved. It seems likely that, had someone asked him, Tertullian would have said that Jesus has paid the debt we owed to God. A passage implies this: "Who has redeemed another's death by his own, but the Son of God alone?"[4] The Latin here does seem to have the connotation of payment, but in many other passages Tertullian appears to interpret the work of Christ in a way similar to Irenaeus' interpretation (which will be expounded later). Nor should that surprise us, for it is clear that Tertullian had read Irenaeus, and in any case, at least on this point, the theology of the bishop of Lyon represented the general consensus of the church at the time.

Tertullian's Christology, like his trinitarian doctrine, is remarkable because he is the first to employ the terms which eventually became the hallmark of orthodoxy: two natures, or substances, in one person.[5] Once again, Tertullian seems to use those terms in a legal sense, rather than in the metaphysical sense they eventually were given.

In reading Tertullian's works as a whole, it is clear that a great deal of the significance of Jesus has to do with his work as a lawgiver.[6] For Tertullian, Jesus is a new Moses and the gospel a new law.[7] Therefore, Jesus' main purpose was to give us the law of repentance. According to that law, anyone who repents, is baptized, and sins no more, will be saved.

From this perspective, baptism is the act that seals repentance and also washes the sinner. But in order to receive baptism, repentance is necessary.[8] In submitting to that rite, commanded by Christ, the repentant sinner receives forgiveness of sins. After that point, one must take care to sin no more, for that would be an insult to the divine majesty. Since baptism cannot be repeated, before requesting that it be administered, Christians must make sure they truly do fear the Lord. For this reason Tertullian felt that baptism should be postponed until the candidate has left behind the dangers and temptations of youth. (Note that his reason for opposing the baptism of children was not that he considered such baptism invalid. On the contrary, it was precisely because he considered it valid and therefore unrepeatable that he opposed it.)

After that first baptism with water, a Christian who sins has the opportunity for one more final act of repentance.[9] After that, however, there is no recourse other than baptism by blood—that is, martyrdom.[10] Like many other Christians of his time, Tertullian believed that God did forgive fallen Christians who later gave witness to their faith and repentance through martyrdom.

It is significant that Tertullian sees baptism as the beginning of the Christian life.[11] After being baptized, Christians are committed not to sin, and for this reason Tertullian opposes the baptism of all who still have temptations ahead—the single, and the widowed who are not yet "more fully strengthened for continence, as well as children."[12] The fact that the rite has exhausted its effective power also is significant, because we shall see that from the perspective of Type C, baptism, although administered only once, continues to be effective throughout life.

This view of baptism as an initial washing away of sins leads us to consider a closely connected question, which became crucial for this entire theological tradition, both before and after Tertullian's time—the question of postbaptismal sins. Toward the middle of the second century in Rome, Hermas, a Christian writer and prophet whose brother was bishop of that city, posed the same question. This became critical because, during a time of persecution, some Christians who had yielded to pressure and fear later wished to rejoin the church. Since they were already baptized, it was not possible for them to take refuge under the repentance of baptism, which supposedly washed away all previous sins. Were such people then entirely out of reach of God's grace? For Hermas this was also a personal question, since he felt guilty because, after having received baptism, he had lusted after a woman. His final decision was that, even after baptism, there was one more opportunity to repent, but that those who sinned after that second repentance "will hardly be saved."[13]

Similar ideas are found in the Second Epistle of Clement,[14] probably written in Rome at about the same time. Later on we shall see how the Type A tradition, which follows Tertullian's perspective and whose forerunners were Hermas and Second Clement, eventually led to the development of the penitential system against which Luther and his followers protested. Thus from a very early date, the question of postbaptismal sin became paramount within the legalistic perspective characteristic of Type A theology.

Tertullian says little about the meaning of communion;[15] he seems to believe it contains nourishment to strengthen Christians in their resolve to be faithful to their baptismal vows.[16]

Finally, we turn to Tertullian's eschatology. In one or two passages, he seems to refer to what would later be known as purgatory.[17] His references are so brief that it is impossible to ascertain the exact meaning of his words, and therefore historians do not agree as to their interpretation, though there is no doubt that the doctrine of purgatory would fit perfectly within the framework of his theology. If we are debtors before God, if each sin committed after baptism somehow contributes to that debt, and if our final destiny depends upon paying that debt, it is logical to conclude that those who die in the faith, but without being able to offer satisfaction for all their sins, will have an opportunity to purge them before going on to their final reward. Once again, Tertullian suggests such a possibility in passing, and even then not clearly. But later theology, following the perspective of Type A to its logical conclusion, affirmed that there is indeed a purgatory and made this an official doctrine of the church and part of the penitential system.

According to Tertullian, the way of salvation will end after the millennium, when God resurrects and judges the entire human race. Some will go to eternal punishment, and the just will receive their reward, being "with God forever." Order will be restored, and all will obey the divine commandment.[18]

As for Tertullian himself, after having defended Christian orthodoxy against pagans and heretics alike, he left the larger church to join the Montanists, whom other Christians regarded as heretics. Montanism was, among other things,[19] a moral rigorism which claimed that, after the "law of the gospel," there was another, even higher—the "law of the Spirit." Tertullian was distressed by the moral lassitude of many Christians and by the apparent willingness of the church at large to accept such sinners in its midst. If the gospel is a new law, it follows that a church that does not fully obey it is not the church of Christ. Because of both temperament and theological conviction, Tertullian felt the need for more moral rigor, and the Montanists offered precisely

that. Some ancient writers assert that he later abandoned
Montanism to found his own sect, which they call "Tertullianist."
Be that as it may, such a final step would be perfectly compatible
with all we know about the great Carthaginian writer.

Type B—The way of salvation appears very different from
the **Alexandrine** perspective. On the basis of what has been said
earlier, it should be clear that for this type of theology, the
human predicament does not consist primarily in owing a debt
that must be satisfied, but in our inability to contemplate God
and thus reflect the divine image, since that is the purpose for
which we were created.[20] Although this does not mean that
Clement and Origen ignore the other dimensions of sin, in
reading their works one receives the impression that our main
difficulty as human beings is that we are in need of illumination
from on high. As in the entire Platonic tradition, such
illumination is not purely rational, but includes an affective
dimension. The illumination we need is a vision of spiritual
realities, a vision that will move our will.[21]

Having clarified the wide meaning of *illumination* within this
context, it is correct to say that Type B theology sees our
ignorance as the primary problem—not our lack of knowledge
of the world, but our lack of the necessary vision, the
illumination, to return to the contemplation of the One, and
thus to our heavenly home. The human creature is eminently
intellectual. Before the Fall, all of us were pure intellects, and the
fact that we are now souls that have bodies is the result of sin, of
having strayed from the contemplation of the Eternal.[22]

This is why Origen can say that the "futility" to which creation
is subject is bodily existence.[23] Bodies are indeed God's
creation—and on this point Origen categorically rejects the
views of the Gnostics. But bodies are creatures of God in
response to the sin of the intellect. Without sin, there would have
been no material creation. And in the end, there once again will
be no material creation.

To human beings, God has sent Jesus Christ, the incarnate
Word, or Logos, of God. Jesus' main function in the process of
salvation is to convey our needed illumination. Origen explains
this through the example of a colossal statue.[24] God's immensity,

when compared to our finitude, is such that we cannot comprehend it. Our position is similar to that of an ant that tries to comprehend a great statue. What we see overawes us but does not move us. If the ant were presented with a smaller statue just like the larger one, but of dimensions more adequate to that insect, the ant would find it easier to see and comprehend it, and thus to be moved by it. The incarnation of the Word in Jesus provides us with that other statue—a faithful image of the larger one, but more adequate to our understanding. Those who see Jesus see the Father, but in a manner befitting the limits of the human intellect. His presence calls us back to the contemplation of the One or, in other words, provides the illumination of which we stood in need.[25]

This theology centers on the divinity of Christ—although, of course, without denying his humanity. For Origen, and for his forerunner Clement of Alexandria, it is important that Jesus be the true image of the Father, so that in seeing him we may be able to see the Father and thus have a true revelation of the Eternal. Since by his time most Christians had categorically rejected the notion that Christ had no physical body, both Clement and Origen affirm the reality of that body. Yet in reading their various works, one receives the impression that the humanity of Christ is necessary only as an instrument whereby the Word is made visible and can thus be our teacher and illuminator.[26]

Origen understands the union of divinity and humanity in Christ as follows: In order to appear in the world, the Word of God was united to an intellect that had not fallen—that is, to a soul like ours but without sin—and a physical body like ours. This is significant because later Alexandrine theology, whose inspiration was derived to a great degree from Origen, emphasized divinity to such a point that the Savior's humanity was endangered, and some of the main theologians of that school denied that Jesus had a human soul. Although Origen did affirm that Jesus had a human soul,[27] and in that respect cannot be blamed for the later course of Alexandrine theology, he did contribute to that course by his emphasis on the divinity of the Savior as the primary contributor to our salvation—which in turn flowed from Origen's understanding of salvation as illumination.

If the work of Christ consists primarily in an illumination, it follows that the sacraments have a similar function. Both baptism and the eucharist are symbols of spiritual realities. Origen acknowledges that this explanation does not agree with what most Christians in his time believe, and therefore says that the symbolic interpretation of the sacraments is the most correct, but that only the enlightened understand this.[28] The popular interpretation, which sees real efficacy in the sacraments, is also acceptable, although less valid.

Probably the most interesting point in Origen's theology is his understanding of the goal of salvation. He believed that in the beginning, creation was purely spiritual. Physical creation is the result of the sin of the pure intellects which God first created. In the end, there will be a total restoration, so that the end will be just like the beginning. Through Jesus Christ, the Holy Spirit, and the church, God is now calling creation back to its original intellectual reality. When the divine purposes are fulfilled the material creation will cease to exist, and all spirits will return to their original state—although before they reach that condition, souls will need to be trained in paradise, which is "a school of souls."[29]

According to Origen, that final restoration will be universal. All intellectual beings, including the demons, will be part of it. In the final analysis, demons are simply intellectual beings, originally created equal to angels and human beings, but whose fall was even more drastic than ours. In the end, all fallen spirits, together with the demons and others who never fell, will once more rejoice in the contemplation of the Eternal.

What can one then say about Hell? It is not an eternal punishment, but the means whereby God purifies fallen spirits, just as the physician uses fire to purify instruments.[30] Even though they must pass through Hell, in the end the demons and unbelievers will return to their original condition.

Furthermore, since the state of the restored creation will be the same as that of the purely spiritual creation of the beginning,[31] what will prevent some intellects from falling again, thus opening a new cycle of fall and restoration? Nothing, and therefore Origen says there may have been other worlds before ours, and there may be others afterward—although he is certain that Jesus suffered once and for all and will not need to suffer in any coming worlds.[32]

Type C—Irenaeus sees all these matters in a very different way. The human predicament is not that we owe a debt because of sin, nor that we stand in need of illumination from on high, but rather that we are subject to Satan.[33] Since humankind stands in solidarity, in Adam's sin we all have sinned, and jointly with him we all have been made slaves of Satan.[34] He is the tyrant who keeps us from acting freely and impedes the human growth God had intended.

After sin, history has continued to move on. The fact that there is history and development is not the result of sin, since God always intended that we should grow in communion with the divine, through a historical process. The course history has actually taken is indeed the result of sin. While we have continued our natural development, which was God's gift, that development has been twisted, so that in a certain sense we all are monstrous. It is as if we had been children who, due to an unfortunate accident, had lost mental ability and the capacity to speak, but still continued to grow.[35] Growth itself is good; but the form it now takes due to that accident is twisted. Likewise, as God's creatures, our development, both as individuals and as a race, is good. But the concrete course of that development is in fact monstrous, because it has been twisted by sin. We are slaves of Satan, just as the child would be enslaved by the accident.

What we need, then, is liberation. We need someone to overcome the tyrant who holds us under subjection, to allow us to become once again the creatures God intended. And after that liberation, we need God to guide us in our renewed growth toward greater communion with the Creator.

For these reasons, Irenaeus describes the main work of Christ as victory against the powers that held us in subjection. "For he called all men that mourn; and granting forgiveness to those who had been led into captivity by their sins, He loosed them from their chains."[36] "He set Himself forth, who had restored liberty to men, and bestowed on them the inheritance of incorruption."[37]

> For he fought and conquered; for He was contending for the
> fathers [perhaps a better translation would be "for the parents,"
> Adam and Eve], and through obedience doing away with
> disobedience completely: for He bound the strong man, and set
> free the weak, and endowed His own handiwork with salvation,
> by destroying sin. . . .
>
> He caused man (human nature) to cleave to and to become one
> with God. For unless man had overcome the enemy of man, the
> enemy would not have been legitimately vanquished. And again:
> unless it had been God who had freely given salvation, we could
> never have possessed it securely.[38]

Jesus accomplished this by turning himself over to the power of
Satan and coming out as conqueror. The work of Christ consisted
precisely in becoming like one of the descendants of Adam and
Eve and not being overcome by the powers of evil.

For this reason, Irenaeus does not focus on the cross as the
entire redemptive work of Christ. For him the cross is important,
but it does not overshadow the incarnation and the resurrection.[39]

What took place in the incarnation was, in a way, what God
had intended from the beginning.[40] The divine and the human
were forever bound into one. This was always part of God's
purpose. Now, because of sin, the incarnation has an added
redemptive dimension. Jesus is the New Adam, the beginning of
a new humanity that is not subject to Satan. Jesus "recapitulates"
(literally, re-heads) humanity.[41] His life is like a new creation, and
this is why he is called the New Adam, an undoing of what was
done when the first creation fell. This is why he needed to live an
entire human life, from childhood to maturity, and in each of
those stages undo the evil that had been done. This is one of the
most prominent themes in Irenaeus' theology, and one that has
drawn the attention of many scholars. It is important to keep in
mind that by *recapitulatio* Irenaeus means both the redoing of
human history, which undoes the work of Satan,[42] and the
forming of a new humanity under a new head.[43] The two are
closely related.

When the life of Jesus led to the cross and the powers of evil
believed they conquered, the Lord rose again, thus destroying

the powers and opening for us, his followers, the gap through which we too can escape from bondage.

Just as we all are sinners because we are members of a body of humanity whose head was the first Adam, so our liberation from the powers of evil is due to our being part of a new creation, a new body whose head is Jesus. Through his incarnation, life, death, and resurrection, Christ has become the New Adam—which he already was, since Adam was modeled from the image of Christ—the head of the new humanity, the church.

Irenaeus understands the image of the church as the body of Christ in a very real way, one that makes a profoundly soteriological statement. Most of us, were we questioned as to the meaning of that image, probably would say that it means we are the instruments the Lord uses to carry forth the divine purpose. However, this is largely a reflection of the pragmatism of our society, which makes us see images such as that of the church being the body of Christ in a functionalist way. Irenaeus takes that image in a deeper, more literal meaning. The fact that we are the body of Christ is precisely the reason we are partakers of his victory. In a passage which seeks to expound the significance of the Lord's resurrection, Irenaeus says that the head of the new humanity has already arisen from among the dead, and therefore, at the proper time, we, the rest of the body, also will arise. The unity between head and body is such that the victory of one is shared by the other.[44]

The meaning of "a new creation" is basically the same. Jesus Christ has begun "afresh the human race."[45] He is the New Adam because in him a new humanity has been inaugurated, so those who are in Christ are "a new creation."[46] In Adam, the old creation was made subject to Satan and therefore to sin and death. In Jesus Christ, the New Adam, the new creation, is victorious over those powers of evil.

As to the manner in which the incarnation takes place, Irenaeus gives no hint of being concerned over issues having to do with how divinity can be joined to humanity, which later shook the church in endless debate. There is no doubt in his mind that Jesus is at once human and divine, but he does not discuss how such a thing is possible: "But in every respect, too,

He is man, the formation of God; and thus took up man into Himself, the invisible becoming visible, the impassible becoming capable of suffering, and the Word being made man, thus summing up all things in Himself."[47]

Irenaeus can speak in such terms without seeming to be concerned about how the divine can become human partly because, for him, divinity and humanity are perfectly compatible, since humanity was made for communion with the divine. From the perspective of Type B, which conceives of the divine in terms of absolute contrast with all human characteristics, the incarnation becomes a logical impossibility. Irenaeus does not think in such terms. For him, God's purpose, from the very beginning, was to become human—if not to save humankind, then to enjoy full communion with it. Therefore Irenaeus sees the incarnation as the culmination of the divine purpose. This does not make it less mysterious, but it certainly avoids seeing the incarnation in terms of logical contradiction. Furthermore, Irenaeus' discussion of the two natures in Christ is usually based on the fact that Christ is the Savior, the conqueror, the founder of a new humanity, the head of a new body.

> For it was to this end that the Word of God became man, and He who was the Son of God became the Son of man, that man, having been taken into the Word, and receiving the adoption, might become the son of God. For by no other means could we have attained incorruptibility and immortality, unless we had been united to incorruptibility and immortality. But how could we be joined to incorruptibility and immortality, unless, first, incorruptibility and immortality had become that which we are also, so that the corruptible might be swallowed by incorruptibility, and the mortal by immortality, that we might receive the adoption of sons?[48]
>
> This took place . . . the Word remaining quiescent, that He might be capable of being tempted, dishonoured, crucified, and of suffering death, but the human nature being swallowed up in it (the divine), when it conquered, and endured [without yielding], and performed acts of kindness, and rose again, and was received up.[49]

In summary, the work of Christ, of which the union of the divine and the human is the center, consists in overcoming the powers of evil and liberating us from their sway, and in joining us to the new Head by making us members of the body of the new creation.

This, in part, is the meaning of baptism.[50] That rite is not simply a washing, a point of departure for the Christian life. It is also, and above all, the means by which we are united to Christ. Baptism is a grafting which makes us branches of the True Vine, members of the body of Christ. It is precisely because of that grafting that we say that our sins are washed away at baptism: not because the water washes us, but because by virtue of our union with Christ, we are now partakers of his victory and therefore freed from the power of sin and from the subjection of the old creation. Therefore, baptism is much more than the beginning point of Christian life. It is valid throughout life, just as a grafting continues to give life to the branch. Through baptism, we are members of the body of Christ—both at the beginning of our Christian life and through its entire duration.

If baptism is a grafting that makes us members of the body of Christ, communion is the means God gives us to be nourished as members of that body.[51] A grafted member lives by the blood and nourishment it receives from the body. Likewise, the Christian is nourished through communion, which at the time of Irenaeus—and throughout most of the history of the church— was the normal worship service of Christians. Thus, Irenaeus is saying that believers are nourished in worship, which is essentially the Eucharist. What communion symbolizes, or, as in later theology, the manner of Christ's presence in it, is not important to him. For Irenaeus, it is crucial that, in partaking of the elements, our union with the head of the body of which we are members is strengthened, and therefore our participation in Christ's victory is renewed.

Perhaps the most interesting point in Irenaeus' theology is his conception of the final goal of human existence. As we have seen, to create humankind, God used as a model the Word who was to be incarnate, because the final goal of human life is to be in communion with the Creator. God's purpose was that Adam and

Eve would grow in justice and in the knowledge of God, so that they would be ever closer to the Creator—a process which continues into eternity.[52]

Irenaeus calls this process "divinization,"[53] and later theologians, particularly in the West, have tended to consider this an undue speculation, reminiscent of Oriental mystical trends which see the goal of human life as a return to the divine, where the human is lost in God. This is not what Irenaeus understands by *divinization*. For him, the distance between God and the human creature is such that no matter how close we approach to the divine, we shall still be creatures and will not be confused with God. The distinction between creature and Creator is never obliterated. Irenaeus actually means that God's purpose is that human beings will grow eternally, ever approaching their Creator, ever having closer communion with God. We were made so that we might "become like gods."

These words, addressed by the Serpent to Adam and Eve in the garden, were a temptation—not because they included an improper ambition, but because human creatures, made by God "like little children," were not ready for such a momentous step. The temptation was to try to foreshorten the divine plan. The Serpent's words, although premature, reflected God's very plan, as is shown in our later becoming God's adoptive children.

The divinization that is the goal of human life thus consists in being the adopted children of God and increasingly resembling our Creator. The gift of immortality is part of that divinization. The same is true of the way God informs our mind, progressively bringing it into agreement with the divine purposes.

A great deal of this may very well seem like undue speculation. However, what must be emphasized here is that Irenaeus' theology does not follow the common expedient of exalting God by denying all value to the human creature. On the contrary, Irenaeus seems to believe that the more he exalts the value of human beings, the more their Creator will be exalted. Part of the great difference between the life of sin and the new creation is that the former is life in subjection, which does not allow us to develop fully, whereas the latter is a life of constant growth, in which our potential is increasingly brought to fruition.

God's purposes include not only the spiritual creation, but also the material. Irenaeus was convinced that, as part of the process of salvation, there will be an earthly kingdom "which is the commencement of incorruption, by means of which kingdom those who shall be worthy are accustomed gradually to partake of the divine nature."[54] Part of that training is a reversal of the present order of power, "that in the creation in which they enjoyed servitude . . . they should reign. . . . It is fitting, therefore, that the creation itself, being restored to its primeval condition, should without restraint be under the dominion of the righteous."[55] These views, usually dubbed "chiliastic" (millenarian), were shared by many Christians in Asia Minor, notably the author of Revelation and Bishop Papias of Hierapolis, who claimed that the Lord had promised an earthly kingdom of enormous abundance.[56] When these views fell into disfavor, Irenaeus and those who held them also fell into general disrepute.

In any case, Irenaeus' vision of the final consummation—and even these words are a misnomer—is not simply a return to the original state, as in Type B, nor even the establishment of a static order, as in Type A, but the vision of a new reality and a new order, a "Kingdom without end,"[57] a kingdom in which all shall be coheirs of the Sovereign and continue to exist and grow in freedom, justice, and communion with God.

On the basis of the foregoing, we can now add to our chart (see p. 64).

The Three Types

	A	B	C
Three Areas	Carthage	Alexandria	Asia Minor and Syria
Three Theologians	Tertullian	Origen	Irenaeus
Main Interest	Moral	Metaphysical	Pastoral
Main Category	Law	Truth	History
Philosophical Orientation	Stoic	Platonic	None in particular
Forerunners	Clement of Rome Hermas Second Clement	Philo (Justin) Clement of Alexandria	Ignatius Polycarp Theophilus
God	Lawgiver Judge	Ineffable One Transcendent	Shepherd Father
Creation	Complete	Originally spiritual Double	Begun
Sin	Breaking the Law	Not contemplating the One	Anticipatory disobedience
Original Sin	Inherited	Individual	One sinned for all (human solidarity)
Human Predicament	Moral debt	Forgetfulness Obfuscation	Subjection
Work of Christ	Expiation Forgiveness New law	Example Teaching Illumination	Victory Liberation Opening the future
Sacraments	Washing Merit	Reminders Symbols	Grafting Nutrition
Final Consummation	Kingdom of law and order	Contemplation Return	Kingdom of freedom and growth

IV

The Use of Scripture

The history of Christian thought may be said to be, in essence, the history of Christian biblical interpretation. Therefore it may be helpful to look at our three types from the perspective of their use of Scripture. We must remember that the theologians we are studying lived at the time the canon of the New Testament was being formed. Irenaeus argued forcibly for the inclusion of the Fourth Gospel, an indication that its authority was still a matter of debate—although it is necessary to point out that he was arguing against the heretics, not against orthodox Christians who did not accept this particular Gospel.[1] All our writers faced Gnostic and other sects which put forth their own written gospels, sometimes attributed to an apostle.

At the same time, even the authority of the Hebrew Scriptures—the Old Testament—was in doubt, for many among the heretics claimed they were the work of a lesser God or that they represented the principle of evil. Therefore, all our theologians needed to find ways to show the relationship between those Scriptures and the Christian faith.

Type A—Tertullian comes to Scripture with the basic attitude of a lawyer who studies a legal text. A clear instance can be seen in his treatise titled *Prescription Against Heretics*. He was concerned over the multitude of heresies circulating at that time. Some claimed that this world was not the creation of God, but of some lesser or evil power. Others added that, since flesh belongs to that evil power, Jesus could not have come in the flesh, and his body therefore was some sort of heavenly substance or a miraculous apparition. Secret teachings received from an apostle were said to be the basis for some of these theories. Others followed the lore of magic and astrology. Most combined several of these doctrines in their own particular fashion.

All three types of theology rejected such doctrines, each in its own way. Tertullian, in his *Prescription Against Heretics,* follows the legal argument to which we referred in chapter 1. Before engaging in any discussion with these heretics as to how Scripture is to be interpreted, says Tertullian, one must ask the previous question—whether heretics have the right to base their arguments on Scripture.[2] At this point, his argument follows the pattern of the lawyer who tries to win a case by showing that the opposition has not grounded its case on proper legal bases, or that the court has no jurisdiction. If the advocate can show that for some reason the opposition has no right to appeal to a certain law, the case is thrown out of court. Likewise, Tertullian claims that Scripture—which to him is essentially a legal text—cannot be used by the heretics. The church has been using the Bible for years without anyone disputing its possession. Furthermore, part of the Bible was written by the church and thus belongs to it. Therefore, the heretics have no right to use the Scripture, and any discussion with them as to the proper interpretation of a biblical text is unnecessary.[3]

In this particular case, and in his entire theological work, Tertullian approaches Scripture after the fashion of a lawyer. Actually, one of his characteristic ways to refer to the Bible is as an "instrument"[4]—a term which has the same legal connotations in Latin as in English, where it may refer to "a legal document (as a deed, will, bond, lease, agreement, mortgage, note, power of attorney, ticket on carrier, bill of lading, insurance policy, warrant, writ) evidencing legal rights or duties, esp. of one party to another."[5] From this perspective, Tertullian can refer to the Old Testament as "the law of Moses," and to the New as "the law of the Gospel."[6]

This in turn means that in the interpretation of Scripture, one is to employ the same methods used in the interpretation of legal texts. We have noted that Tertullian's theological treatises and his arguments within such treatises often follow the rhetorical structures in which advocates were trained. When applied in a court of law, these methods require that the interpreter abide by the literal meaning of the text. While allegorical interpretation may have its place as a flourish in the discourse, the argument itself must be based on what the law actually says.

Following these methods, Tertullian seeks two things in Scripture: He seeks first of all the laws and commandments that will show what God demands and expects of human beings; he also seeks prophecies that will serve to confirm his interpretation of those laws.

As to prophecy, this method of biblical interpretation is not Tertullian's creation, for it has ancient roots in both Hebrew and Christian tradition. However, in Tertullian's works, prophecy gains a special place, both by its importance and by its meaning. Its importance is such that Tertullian tends to reduce the Old Testament—apart from the Law—to prophecies about the New Testament; and in the New he sees most of all a series of prophecies about a new law that will supersede even that of the gospel.[7] He tends to limit the function of the prophet to prediction of the future and forgets that in the Bible the "prophet" is one who speaks in God's name and that prediction of the future is only an incidental element in that function.

In order to understand the use Tertullian makes of Old Testament prophecy, it is helpful to remember that most of his works are polemical in character. In trying to prove to the Jews that Jesus was the long-awaited Messiah, it was natural to refer to the ancient messianic prophecies—as had been done earlier by Justin and others as early as the writers of the New Testament, and probably even before. On the other hand, when Marcion claimed that the God of the Old Testament had nothing to do with the Father of Jesus, the prophetic argument now served to show that the Old Testament was the Word of the same God who sent Jesus, rather than that Jesus was the Messiah.[8]

Once again, there is no doubt that there is a great deal in the New Testament that refers to the future. The eschatological dimension is central to the New Testament. Tertullian, however, tends to interpret those texts as meaning that what he calls "the law of the Gospel" is to pass, and at a future time—that is, Tertullian's time—a new age will begin, with a superior law, no longer that of the gospel but of the Spirit. It was this view of the New Testament that led Tertullian, the old champion of orthodoxy against all sorts of heresy, to abandon the larger church and become a Montanist. His interpretation of Scripture as a legal text, in which one seeks a passage or phrase which applies to each situation, led him to take that step.

On the other hand, we have said that in Scripture, Tertullian sees not only prophecy, but law. The fundamental theme of his theology is moral in character. His primary question is, What does God require of us? Since the Bible is the Word of God, who is above all a legislator, the Bible must be, first of all, legislation. As could be expected, Tertullian finds a basis for this position in those books of the Old Testament that are clearly legal in character. However, this sort of interpretation runs into difficulties when it must deal with the historical books of the Old Testament, of which Tertullian makes relatively little use.[9]

When it comes to the New Testament, Tertullian refers to the gospel as the "law of Christ." What he sees as having taken place in the advent of Jesus is that the old law has been abrogated—not because Jesus has fulfilled it or because we are under grace, but because we are under a new and harsher law. Mosaic law was a "figure" or "shadow" of the law to come,[10] and for that reason has been superseded. The new law which God has given to Christians is essentially the same as the old law, although much more strict. It is thus that Tertullian interprets the words of Jesus in the Sermon on the Mount: "But I say unto you."[11]

The consequence of all this is a rigid, literalist, moralizing reading of Scripture. This certainly is not the entire picture, for there are in Tertullian's writings passages which show a deeper and more dynamic understanding of Scripture. At this point, the reader would do well to remember the need not to read our discussion of the three types as a literal description of the entire theological system of these theologians. Having said this, however, it is also necessary to insist that in Type A theology, the Bible has a twofold function: (a) as a proof of Christian orthodoxy (which is the principal use of prophecy in this context); and (b) as a guidebook to tell us what we are to do in order to please God and reach heaven.

Type B—Origen approaches Scripture with a completely different attitude.[12] As we saw in chapter 1, he seeks first the eternal truths, although he does find rules of conduct. Since eternal truths must not depend on what happens within the passing sphere of time, but must be anterior to all events, Origen seeks in Scripture a way to penetrate beyond the temporal and passing, and reach the immutable.[13] His interest lies in going beyond what the biblical text says about historical events, and finding the ultimate meaning which lurks behind the text.

Origen holds that the biblical text usually has at least two meanings: one literal and one spiritual. On occasion he becomes enthused with a text and expounds a multitude of meanings, hidden at various levels. However, it suffices to say that in general, any biblical text has at least a literal meaning and a deeper spiritual significance. The literal meaning is not to be rejected, except in those cases in which it would seem to imply something unworthy of God—for instance, that God walked in the garden taking the breeze. Yet, even in cases where the literal meaning is not to be rejected, it remains an inferior meaning, addressed to those who are ignorant or less intelligent.[14] Those who remain at that level are accused by Origen of Judaizing tendencies, for he claims that the reason the Jews did not accept the gospel was their literalistic frame of mind in interpreting their own Scriptures.[15]

Over and beyond the literal meaning, the spiritual one opens vast horizons to the wise Christian. While there are texts the literal meaning of which must be rejected, all texts do have a spiritual meaning. It is here that the wise believer discovers those higher truths the common believer cannot discover, precisely because the latter remains at the level of the literal meaning.

How are we to discover that spiritual meaning? Origen never offers clear directions.[16] He often seems to be employing the same methods of interpretation used by some of his pagan contemporaries in the interpretation of classical Greek literature. Since the religious and philosophical outlook of the Mediterranean world had evolved a great deal since Homer, many were not disposed to accept literally what he and others had said about the gods and related subjects. To respond to such objections without diminishing the value of the classics, some had recourse to allegorical interpretation.[17] Origen then followed the same path with reference to Scripture: It is to be interpreted allegorically, in such a fashion that it may be shown to agree with the best elements in philosophy. This was not a radically new departure, for earlier, also in Alexandria, the Jew Philo and the Christian Clement had interpreted Scripture in that manner.[18]

Allegorical interpretation seeks to discover a symbolic meaning in a text. That meaning is to be found not only in the text as a whole, but also in each of its parts. Thus, for instance, the texts in which God commands utter destruction of the enemy, or in which the just rejoice in such destruction, actually refer to the need to destroy the vices of the soul:

> If I must now explain how the just man "slays his enemies," and prevails everywhere, it is to be observed that, when he says, "Every morning will I destroy the wicked of the land, that I may cut off all workers of iniquity from the city of Jehovah," by "the land" he means the flesh whose lusts are at enmity with God; and by "the city of Jehovah" he designates his own soul, in which was the temple of God, containing the true idea and conception of God, which makes it to be admired by all who look upon it. As soon then, as the rays of the Sun of righteousness shine into his soul, feeling strengthened and invigorated by their influence, he sets himself to destroy all the lusts of the flesh, which are called "the wicked of the land," and drives out of that city of the Lord which is his soul all thoughts which work iniquity, and all suggestions which are opposed to the truth. And in this way also the just give up to destruction all their enemies, which are their vices, so that they do not spare even the children, that is, the early beginnings and promptings of evil. In this sense also we understand the language of the 137th Psalm: "O daughter of Babylon, who art to be destroyed; happy shall he be that rewardeth thee as thou hast served us: happy shall he be that taketh and dasheth the little ones against the stones." For the "little ones" of Babylon (which signifies confusion) are those troublesome sinful thoughts which arise in the soul; and he who subdues them by striking, as it were, their heads against the firm and solid strength of reason and truth, is the man who "dasheth the little ones against the stones"; and he is therefore truly

> blessed. God may therefore have commanded men to destroy all
> their vices utterly, even at their birth, without having enjoined
> anything contrary to the teaching of Christ.[19]

This use of Scripture agrees with what we have said about
Origen's fundamental interests. It is important to him to
discover the eternal truths that lie hidden in the symbolism of
the biblical narrative. Although Origen does not seem to have
been familiar with Tertullian's writings, one may surmise, on the
basis of what he says in similar cases, that the Carthaginian's
literalism would have appeared to him very similar to that of
which he accused the Jews, and he would have felt that
Tertullian lacked the spiritual depth of the true Christian
philosopher. Tertullian would have responded that what
Origen sought to discover in the biblical text was too similar to
what the philosophers were saying; that to reach such
conclusions, the Bible was altogether unnecessary.

This is precisely the weak point of allegorical interpretation:
Since it is the interpreter who determines the symbolism to be
found in Scripture, it is also the interpreter who determines,
through the selection of symbols, what the Bible will say. Carried
to an extreme, this method turns the text into a mirror in which
the interpreter's image is reflected. It is for this reason that
Origen the Platonist philosopher has no difficulty finding in
Scripture a Platonist message. As Hanson would say, "The
connection between the original word and the allegory rests on
nothing but the arbitrary decision of the allegorist."[20]

Type C—Finally, **Irenaeus** approaches Scripture in a way
radically different from either Tertullian or Origen. His
fundamental vision is that of a shepherd God, leading his people
through history.

> Thus it was, too, that God formed man at the first, because of His
> munificence; but chose the patriarchs for the sake of their
> salvation, and prepared a people beforehand, teaching the
> headstrong to follow God; and raised up prophets upon earth,
> accustoming man to bear His Spirit {within him}, and to hold
> communion with God: He Himself, indeed, having need of
> nothing, but granting communion with Himself to those who

stood in need of it, and *sketching out, like an architect, the plan of salvation* to those that pleased Him. And He did Himself furnish guidance to those who beheld Him not in Egypt, while to those who became unruly in the desert He promulgated a law very suitable {to their condition}. Then, on the people who entered into the good land He bestowed a noble inheritance; and He killed the fatted calf for those converted to the Father, and presented them with the finest robe. *Thus, in a variety of ways, He adjusted the human race to an agreement with salvation.*[21]

Therefore the biblical narrative must be taken very seriously. It is that narrative which witnesses to the work of God, whose eternal purposes unfold in history. If the Bible becomes no more than an allegory, nothing is left of that work and that witness. Scripture, rather than setting forth a series of eternal truths which could be discovered apart from our historical circumstances or from God's revelation in history, teaches us what Irenaeus calls the divine *oikonomía,*[22] the history of God's relationship with humankind.[23] Therefore, there is progression in the biblical narrative; and there is also continuity. Without progression, history would be no more than a shadow, as is the case in the Platonic tradition. Without continuity, without discernible patterns, history would be meaningless. Irenaeus sees this combination of progression, continuity, and historical concreteness in the Son's ministrations to humanity:

{He} did also show to the human race prophetic visions, and diversities of gifts, and His own ministrations, and the glory of the Father, *in regular order and connection, at the regular time for the benefit [of mankind].* For where there is *a regular succession,* there is also *fixedness;* and where fixedness, there *suitability to the period;* and where suitability, there also *utility.*[24]

In that history, in spite of human sin and the many times the people of God have been disobedient, God has been leading them toward the final consummation. Therefore, there is progression in the biblical narrative, and the Bible is to be interpreted historically.

This means at least three things: First, the events told in the

Bible are to be taken as real, without attempting to dissolve them into allegory whenever they do not fit a given philosophical system. Second, texts that are by their nature allegorical—what Irenaeus calls parables—should be interpreted in the light of texts that are plain, not vice versa.[25] Finally, the events in biblical history are to be understood as part of the entire history of God's actions—the *oikonomía*—and therefore, while historically real, they have a meaning which goes beyond themselves. The first two points establish the difference between Irenaeus' hermeneutics and Origen's. The third precludes Tertullian's legalistic and static literalism.

This sort of scriptural interpretation is usually called typological, because in the events of which the Bible speaks, one is to see "types" or "figures" of later events—especially of Jesus Christ, but also of the church and the final consummation.

Such typological interpretation was not Irenaeus' creation. On the contrary, its roots go back to the New Testament.[26] A few decades before Irenaeus, Justin Martyr declared that God spoke in the Hebrew Scriptures through both "sayings"—*logoi*—and "types" or "figures"—*typoi*.[27] He went on to explain the difference between these in such a way that the "sayings" amount to what are now commonly called "prophecies"—words that foretell the future. "Types," on the other hand, are events or physical realities which in themselves point toward a future event.

Irenaeus agrees with Justin about this twofold manner in which Scripture speaks. Indeed, the very structure of his work *The Demonstration of the Apostolic Preaching* supports this view. The first part of the book gives a number of typological interpretations, whereby the Old Testament points to the New; the latter part is a series of arguments from prophecy. It is to typology—that is, to events by which God's promises are known—that the following passage refers: "However, it is not by means of visions alone which were seen, and words which were proclaimed, but also in actual works, that He was beheld by the prophets, in order that through them He might prefigure and show forth future events beforehand."[28]

In other words, since all history is in God's hands, and God is leading events toward certain goals, there are themes or manners of action which appear repeatedly, although they are never identical. This is what is meant by "succession" and "fixedness" in the passage quoted above. History is not mere repetition, like a wheel endlessly turning on an axis; nor is it capricious, disjointed happenings. As history moves on, with both its newness and its continuity, some themes appear repeatedly, always with variations, but consistently pointing to their fulfillment. Thus Irenaeus' typological hermeneutics do not deny the concreteness and uniqueness of a historical event; nor do they try to transmute that event into an eternal truth.[29] The main characteristic of this approach to biblical interpretation is that a theme can appear again and again, since human history is a single history. But at the same time, that theme is constantly changing, since history moves forward and the divine purposes are being realized. In any case, the history of Israel—and perhaps all of history, although Irenaeus is not clear on this matter—is to be understood typologically.

> Thus, too, He imposed upon the [Jewish] people the construction of the tabernacle, the building of the temple, the election of the Levites, sacrifices also, and oblations, legal monitions, and all the other service of the law. He does Himself truly want {need} none of these things, for He is always full of all good, and had in Himself the odour of all kindness, and every perfume of sweet-smelling savors, even before Moses existed. Moreover, He instructed the people, who were prone to turn to idols, instructing them by repeated appeals to persevere and to serve God, calling them to the things of primary importance by means of those which were secondary; that is, to things that are real, by means of those that are typical {in the sense of being "types"} . . . as Paul also says: "For they drank of the rock which followed them: and the rock was Christ." And again, having first mentioned what are contained in the law, he goes on to say: "Now all these things happened to them in a figure {the Greek says "in type"}; but they were written for our admonition, upon whom the end of the ages is come." For by means of types they learned to fear God, and to continue devoted in His service.[30]

Obviously, what we have here is not only a way of approaching and interpreting Scripture, but a total perspective upon human history. What Irenaeus proposes is not a system of philosophical doctrines, a la Origen, nor a series of moral rules and principles, a la Tertullian, but an entire vision of the world and history in the light of biblical revelation.

Once again, however, a caveat is in order. Presented here is a schematic outline of the characteristic approaches to Scripture of each of the three types we are studying. It would not be difficult to find in each of our authors instances in which they seem to interpret Scripture according to the principles we have attributed to another kind of theology. In particular, if it is true that Type C is older than the other two, we should not be surprised to find typological interpretation in Tertullian, Clement, or Origen.[31] Also, although to a lesser degree, both Tertullian and Irenaeus do on occasion lapse into allegory.[32] In spite of their many differences, our theologians still belonged to the same church and would not have seen each other as heretics.

With this in mind, we can now complete our chart (see p. 76).

The Three Types

	A	B	C
Three Areas	Carthage	Alexandria	Asia Minor and Syria
Three Theologians	Tertullian	Origen	Irenaeus
Main Interest	Moral	Metaphysical	Pastoral
Main Category	Law	Truth	History
Philosophical Orientation	Stoic	Platonic	None in particular
Forerunners	Clement of Rome Hermas Second Clement	Philo (Justin) Clement of Alexandria	Ignatius Polycarp Theophilus
God	Lawgiver Judge	Ineffable One Transcendent	Shepherd Father
Creation	Complete	Originally spiritual Double	Begun
Sin	Breaking the Law	Not contemplating the One	Anticipatory disobedience
Original Sin	Inherited	Individual	One sinned for all (human solidarity)
Human Predicament	Moral debt	Forgetfulness Obfuscation	Subjection
Work of Christ	Expiation Forgiveness New law	Example Teaching Illumination	Victory Liberation Opening the future
Sacraments	Washing Merit	Reminders Symbols	Grafting Nutrition
Final Consummation	Kingdom of law and order	Contemplation Return	Kingdom of freedom and growth
Scriptural Interpretation	Moral code Prophecy	Allegory	Typology Prophecy

V

A Matter of Perspective

Up to this point, we have been expounding and comparing our three types of theology as they found expression in the latter part of the second century. The reader will probably find Type A to be the most familiar, since in many points it corresponds with what we have grown accustomed to view as traditional Christian orthodoxy. Type B is probably less familiar, particularly in its most daring speculative flights—such as the preexistence of souls. But in general, the reader may have found points of contact with various theological systems taught in seminaries and universities in the last two centuries. Type C is probably the most alien to the contemporary Western reader— and that is precisely the reason it seems important to point out that there was this third option in the early church, and to expound on some of its main tenets.

However, were we to limit ourselves to this exposition and comparison of three types of theology, we would be simply following a fairly classical method of theological inquiry—one which derives from the prevalence of Type B in academic circles. This method, which centers on the study of ideas without taking into consideration their sociopolitical setting and hidden agendas, has come under harsh and justified criticism. It ignores the degree to which social and economic agendas, both conscious and hidden, affect theological formulation—an insight that has been reinforced by modern psychological and sociological disciplines.

In order to incorporate this insight into our inquiry, we must go beyond the mere exposition and comparison of the three types. We must ask about the social and economic agendas served by each, even though their main exponents may not have been aware of them. Then we shall be able to understand why

Type C eventually was abandoned in favor of types A and B —and why in our day Type A seems to be dominant in many of our local congregations, while Type B holds sway in colleges and universities.

This makes our inquiry much more difficult. Very little is known of the social and economic circumstances of Christians in the second century, partly because the extant texts do not give sufficient information, and partly because scholars usually have not asked social and economic questions of those texts.[1] The little that is known is not enough to make clear distinctions between possible social agendas in one area as compared with another. Furthermore, given the fragmentary nature of our sources and the lack of reliable statistical data, one can never be certain that a particular source does not reflect an exceptional condition. This means we cannot rely on sociological studies and profiles in the manner we could, for instance, in a study of the rise of fundamentalism or of the social gospel in the United States.

Fortunately, another avenue is open to us. We can look at each of these theologies and ask what sort of social agenda they would serve. We may even be able to connect some items in an agenda with what we know of the circumstances of a particular group in the community where that theology developed. While refraining from any claim that our sources describe the circumstances or social goals of the majority of Christians at that time or in that place, we certainly can seek to discover how a particular theology could serve a social agenda, either of the community within which it took shape or among those who later adopted it.

Thus, we shall not claim that Origen's theology, for instance, reflects or supports the social agenda of the Alexandrine Christian community at large. We simply do not know enough about that community, and what we do know is often contradictory. However, we can make an argument that Origen's theology served the social agenda of that segment of the community with which he identified. Then we can seek to show how similar theologies developed at later times, in places and situations where a similar agenda was present.

For reasons of clarity, which will become apparent, we shall leave our normal order of exposition and begin by directing our attention not at Type A, but at Type B.

Type B—The **Alexandrine** Christian community probably included people of very diverse circumstances. It is not clear that the pagan Celsus wrote in Alexandria; Origen, when he undertook to refute Celsus' *True Word,* knew no more about him than his name and his work. In any case, Origen did not refute Celsus' description of the social status of Christians:

> We see, indeed, in private houses workers in wool and leather, and fullers, and persons of the most uninstructed and rustic character, not venturing to utter a word in the presence of their elders and wise masters; but when they get hold of the children privately, and certain women as ignorant as themselves, they pour forth wonderful statements, to the effect that they ought not to give heed to their father and to their teachers, but should obey them; that the former are foolish and stupid, and neither know nor can perform anything that is really good, being preoccupied with empty trifles; that they alone know how men ought to live, and that, if the children obey them, they will both be happy themselves, and will make their home happy also. And while thus speaking, if they see one of the instructors of youth approaching, or one of the more intelligent class, or even the father himself, the more timid among them become afraid, while the more forward incite the children to throw off the yoke, whispering that in the presence of father and teachers they neither will nor can explain to them any good thing . . . they must leave their father and their instructors, and go with the women and their playfellows to the women's apartments, or to the leather shop, or to the fuller's shop, that they may attain to perfection—and by these words they gain them over.[2]

The fact that Origen was content with calling all this a "calumny," and did not try to show that it was false, would seem to indicate that, in part at least, it may have been a true description of a certain segment of Christianity in Alexandria. In any case, true or not, it is undeniable that Origen did not glory in Christianity's low social status. He was no Tatian, to boast about the "barbarian" nature of his "philosophy."[3] On the contrary, the entire thrust of his theological work is to show that

Christianity is perfectly compatible with the "best" of Greek and Hellenistic philosophy. Celsus' description of "kitchen evangelism" must have hurt Origen to the quick—more so since there was some truth to it. His response was to continue writing his *Against Celsus,* a treatise whose very existence would be clear proof that not all Christian teachers were ignorant workers in wool and leather.

The conflict which produced both Celsus' work and Origen's rebuttal was not new in Alexandria. Indeed, even before Christianity arrived, Jews were accused of being ignorant barbarians who followed a very unphilosophical way of life. Philo and others had sought to respond to such accusations, and now Clement and Origen took up a similar task on behalf of Christianity.

That undertaking was in itself a sign of a certain ambivalence. Philo's work shows that, while he wished to remain faithful to the religion of his elders, he was deeply concerned for his pagan peers' opinion of that religion. He was not particularly interested in converting them, but he wanted to show both them and himself that his religion made sense, that it was compatible with the "best" of the Platonic tradition.

The intellectual difficulties in such an enterprise have often been pointed out, and it is not necessary to dwell on them here. It is clear that the gulf between Platonism and Judaism cannot easily be bridged in a way that is faithful to both.

What must be dwelt upon, however, is the sociopolitical difficulty of such an enterprise. Indeed, the entire Platonic tradition has an aristocratic flavor which has long been acknowledged. From this perspective, philosophy is an occupation for the fortunate superior souls not entangled in the contemplation of material things. Such souls usually inhabit bodies that do not need to worry about their sustenance, for it is somehow provided. Ideally in this tradition, society should be governed by these fortunate few, since "the many," who are engrossed in making a living, do not really know what is best for them and for society.

Over against this opinion, the Hebrew Scriptures speak of God's preferential love for the poor, for "the many" who must labor for their sustenance. What is good for the community is not to be determined by a philosophical or scholarly elite, but is set down as the will of God. Any notion of "wisdom," or of a "philosophical life" not based on doing the will of the God of justice, would be alien to such Scriptures. Therefore, an attempt to yoke Platonic and Hebrew wisdom together risks turning the latter into an aristocratic enterprise for the fortunate few.

In this connection, it is instructive to consider Philo's ambivalent attitude toward wealth. He and his family were quite wealthy—to the point that one of his brothers was able to plate nine gates in the Temple of Jerusalem with gold and silver and also lend a small fortune to Herod Agrippa.[4] At the same time, Philo spoke disparagingly of riches and borrowed on the Stoic and Cynic theme of wisdom as the capacity to set aside the urge for material things. This did not lead him, however, to give up his wealth or social position—in fact, he was quite critical of those "philosophers" who did so and then lived on public charity. He praised those who did not value riches; but he became incensed when the wealthy in the Jewish community of Alexandria were despoiled. Perhaps the best way to describe Philo's social and economic views is that of D. L. Mealand:

> It is true that he was dragged from philosophy to public affairs, when his views of spiritual progress urged him in the opposite direction. But more important is Philo's adherence to a religion some of whose texts reflect the outlook of less privileged groups. Philo's social position was ambiguous. He was wealthy, but also identified with a people who were vulnerable to abuse and sometimes attack.[5]

Christians such as Clement and Origen found themselves and their immediate community in a similar situation. Although probably the majority of Christians in Alexandria still belonged to the lower classes, the new faith was beginning to make inroads among the relatively wealthy and powerful. Clement wrote a treatise, *Who Is the Rich to Be Saved?* in which he allegorized Jesus' words regarding riches and thus made it easier for Christians to retain their wealth. Origen's father, when he died as a martyr, had sufficient wealth to be confiscated by the royal treasurer.

Origen himself then took refuge in the house of a rich Christian woman. Later on his protector, a certain Ambrose, was wealthy enough to provide him with several secretaries. Therefore, although still subject to persecution and technically under various sorts of civil disenfranchisement, part of the Christian community in Alexandria had risen to circumstances similar to those of the Jewish community in Philo's time. This in turn meant that, as in the case of Philo, the opinion of the learned became important, at least for that segment of the church with which Clement and Origen were more closely related.

> A large and rich community, existing in the bosom of a great University town, could not long submit to exclusion from the paramount interests of the place. Their most prominent young men attended the lectures of the heathen professors. . . . It was necessary to recognize, and if possible to profit by, the growing connection between the church and the lecture-room.[6]

It was within this context that Alexandrine Christian theology took shape. Clement and Origen desired to show that their faith was compatible with the surrounding society's idea of the highest achievements of human culture. Since they were adherents of both Christianity and Platonism, they were particularly distressed that Platonists believed Christianity to be intellectually inferior. This may be the reason Origen had so much difficulty in conceding that Celsus was a Platonist—which his *True Word* clearly shows—and insisted on calling him an Epicurean.[7] Alexandrine theology set out to show, both to the pagans and to itself, that there was no reason cultured Platonists should despise Christianity.

This is the task of apologetic theology. Type B theology is essentially apologetic. Both Clement and Origen wrote significant works addressed to the cultured among the despisers, seeking to show that their attitude was based on a misunderstanding, that Christianity was indeed the "true philosophy." Even those works of Clement and Origen that are not, strictly speaking, apologetic, have the same tone. In these one sees faith trying to prove to itself that it is intellectually respectable—one could call them "in-house" apologetics.

The value and achievements of this sort of theology ought not to be underestimated. In the early centuries of the Christian proclamation it performed an important evangelistic role. Such great Christian leaders as Justin Martyr and Gregory the Wonder-worker were brought to faith by apologetics[8]—and there is no way to know how many others followed a similar path.

The problem, however, is the use to which this sort of theology can be put when, beyond being apologetic, it becomes normative. A significant difference exists between saying, with Clement, that philosophy is the handmaiden which leads pagans to faith,[9] then going on to say, also with him, that biblical affirmations about God are to be interpreted in such a way that they do not contradict what philosophy tells us about the Ineffable One.[10] The apologetic bridge that leads unbelievers to faith in one direction, can lead believers to apostasy in the other!

If we return to the basic quest of this chapter, the social and economic agendas served by Type B theology, the answer seems clear. This type draws its initial impetus from a desire to show the compatibility between the Christian faith and the best of Hellenistic philosophy. As such, it serves an evangelistic function. Second, it helps those Christians who are troubled by the low social status and lack of respectability of their faith. But also, it opens the way for an interpretation of Christianity which accommodates the desires of those who are respected in society. This is clear in Clement's treatise, *Who Is the Rich to Be Saved?* In Origen, it is less clear, for he did extol poverty and simplicity above riches. But he did so on the Hellenistic basis of the so-called philosophical life, not on the biblical basis of God's call to justice. For this reason, he sold his library in exchange for a very modest guaranteed income. His praise of poverty was not a call to justice or praise of the poor, but praise for the life of contemplation which those who choose to become poor—but are not needy—can enjoy.

Like Plato's philosophy, the theology of the Alexandrines is essentially elitist. Clement thought of himself and his select circle as "true gnostics"—that is, Christians who really understood the nature of the faith. He clearly felt that "the life of the ordinary believer, that is to say, of the great body of the Church, is a lower life."[11] Such elitism is an essential feature of Type B theology.

> The Alexandrines were aristocratic in their estimate of human nature. Man at his best was their concern, but they had little regard for the crowd. The mixed multitude impedes the escape of the chosen people from bondage. It is a fit parallel to the indiscriminate mob of opinions which hinder the soul in its journey from bondage to the land where truth is found.[12]

There are other, deeper levels at which Type B theology could be used to serve a social agenda. Its static understanding of reality, which it derived from a similar understanding in the Platonist tradition, tended to relieve any pressure on the status quo derived from a vision of God's future order. Its high valuation of the intellectual life, to the detriment of material life, tended to justify a social order in which those who worked with their minds—teachers and scholars, but also administrators and rulers—were placed high above those who provided for the physical sustenance of society, and leisure was considered more dignified than work.

Thanks to this theology, when the Empire decided to embrace Christianity, much of the groundwork had been laid for that momentous step. People of the higher classes could join the church with a sense that they were not abandoning the best achievements of their class and culture. It was now possible to interpret Christianity as a highly sophisticated philosophy, perfectly suited for the sophisticated in the Empire. Their leisure, based on the labor of others, could now be seen as leading to the superior life of contemplation. All this, rather than its intrinsic power or its faithfulness to the gospel, was the main reason Type B theology gained a very significant role in the history of Christian thought, and why successive variations of it have appeared at different times.

Type A—In the case of **Tertullian** and Type A theology, the situation is more difficult to describe. For one thing, we know even less about the social conditions of Christians in Carthage in the late second century than we do about those in Alexandria.

Furthermore, in Carthage there was no longstanding theological tradition on which we can draw, as was the case in Alexandria.

There are some indications that Christianity in North Africa was beginning to draw followers who had at least moderate means. Tertullian, who wrote his first treatises in Greek and was a master of the rhetorical use of Latin, had clearly received an excellent education and did not belong to the lower classes. Indeed, his father was a centurion of the proconsular cohort; the family belonged to that intermediate echelon of Roman administration which, in some ways, was the backbone of the Empire. The *Martyrdom of Perpetua and Felicitas* also indicates that Christians had made some inroads among the well-to-do,[13] and since Tertullian did declare that wealth could be good if used in good causes,[14] it would seem there were at least some among the Christians in his community who had a measure of wealth. Those who were tempted to buy off the authorities in time of persecution[15] must have had the means to do so. Also, there were those who, according to Tertullian, were capable of being tempted by the vice of "immoderate having."[16]

As one reads the apologetic works of Tertullian and other writers of the area—Minucius Felix, Cyprian, Lactantius, even Augustine—it becomes apparent that the main accusation Christians faced was not that they were ignorant, but that they were immoral, licentious, even subversive. In Tertullian's *Apology* and in the *Octavius* of Minucius Felix, the main argument is not against learned detractors of Christianity, but against accusations that Christians ate children and practiced ceremonial incest.[17] Tertullian, Minucius Felix, and later Cyprian in his treatise *To Demetrianus* and Augustine in *The City of God,* were forced to deal with the charge that the gods had made Rome great and that the various calamities which befell the Empire were due to the impiety of Christians in abandoning the traditional gods—in other words, Christians were accused of subversion on a cosmic level.[18]

Given these contexts and circumstances, Tertullian's response was diametrically opposed to that of the Alexandrines. While the latter sought to reconcile the Christian faith with Hellenistic philosophy, Tertullian would have nothing to do with such reconciliation. He saw the two as natural enemies. Indeed, the attempt to bring them together seemed to him the ultimate source of most heresies. For these reasons, and for his scathing criticism of a great deal of what went on around him, Tertullian has been used as a prime example of what H. Richard Niebuhr called the "Christ against culture" approach.

On the other hand, Tertullian's position was not that simple, for he too was concerned about the notion of Christianity held by the respectable people around him. Therefore, the difference between types A and B on the question of apologetics is one of tone and emphasis more than basic outlook. While most of Type B deals with doctrinal matters, most of the work of Tertullian (and later of such successors as Minucius Felix, Cyprian, Lactantius, and Augustine) deals with practical and moral issues. In a schematic way, one could say that, while Clement and Origen were interested in illustrating the truth of Christian doctrine, Tertullian's main interest was to illustrate the rightness of Christian life. Or, going back to the main categories in which we have sought to place these two types of theology, one could say that while the apologetic of Type B is based on truth, that of Type A is based on law. While Clement and Origen sought to show that their faith was compatible with the best of Greek philosophy, Tertullian wished to prove that his was compatible with the best Roman moral achievements.

Here again, the bridges of apologetic turn out to be able to bear traffic in both directions. In one, they serve to open the way to Christian faith for the unbeliever who may be led astray by the rumors circulated about Christian immorality. This was certainly the way Tertullian pursued the apologetic task and the way he intended that it be used. However, in the other direction, this very bridge can be used to turn Christianity into a system of support for the existing moral and legal order. Interpreted as a set of good moral rules to be followed, Christianity could be used to advantage by those who undertook to bolster the order of society.

In a sense, this is precisely what happened after Constantine's reign. Tertullian's faith, which had put him in danger of death at the hands of the authorities, now became the basis on which those authorities demanded obedience and allegiance. This in turn made it easier for the powerful to claim Christianity as their faith, with very little change in the nature and use of their power. Those favored by law and order found support and encouragement in what amounted to a theology of law and order.

Type C—Even less is known about the social milieu of Christians in Lyon, where **Irenaeus** spent most of his adult life, than about that of Alexandria or Carthage. The account of the martyrs of Lyon and Vienne, an incident which took place shortly before Irenaeus became bishop, gives various bits of information that can be pieced together. The names mentioned would seem to indicate that most of the believers were originally from the eastern part of the Empire—probably from the same region in which Irenaeus grew up—but since it is impossible to know the reason for their migration, it is also impossible to determine their social or economic status.[19] Of one, a certain Vittius Epagathus, it is said that he was "a man of distinction."[20] The same document also says that the slaves of some Christians were arrested in an effort to gather evidence against their masters—clear proof that at least some Christians were wealthy enough to possess slaves. At the lower echelon of the social scale, slaves were also among the martyred. (As an aside, it is interesting to note that the document does not list Vettius Epagathus among the martyrs. It is possible also that the author of the document, obviously a survivor, was the master of some of the slaves arrested.)

Irenaeus himself apologizes for his poor use of Greek, offering as an excuse that he is a resident among the Celts and has never studied rhetoric. While the quality of his Greek makes it likely that he intended his reference to the Celts as a literary device, it is true that his works give no indication that he had mastered the classical forms of rhetoric. It is also to be expected that few if any among the converted Celts were people of high standing.

In any case, if it is true that Irenaeus' theology represents the longstanding tradition in Asia Minor and Syria, it is to that area of the Empire that we must look for the background to his thought. Irenaeus grew up with memories of the persecution of Domitian, which gave rise to the book of Revelation. Asia Minor was noted for its enthusiasm for the cult of the emperor, and therefore also for the ensuing difficulties of the Christians.[21] This was the area through which Ignatius had traveled en route to his martyrdom in Rome.

At about the same time, in the northern province of Bythinia, Pliny the Younger had been torturing Christians to learn more about their faith and executing those who refused to abandon it. Irenaeus' own teacher, Polycarp, had died as a martyr. (Was it perhaps to escape such persecution that Irenaeus and others in his congregation fled to Lyon?)

As in other parts of the Empire, the church in Asia Minor and Antioch included fairly well-to-do people as well as slaves and others from the low classes. The one thing they had had in common ever since the times of Paul and other New Testament writers was that they were rejected by the society around them. While not all were poor, it appears that those of more wealth and prominence were, as sociologists would say, people of "high status inconsistency" or "low status crystallization"[22]—that is, people whose wealth or other reasons for high status did not quite counteract other factors which led to lower status. This was a church that entertained no illusions as to the goodness of the social order.

Coming back to Irenaeus, it is clear that his theological agenda is very different from that of the Alexandrines as well as that of Tertullian. He is not interested in making Christianity respectable, on the basis of either philosophy or morality. His writings are not addressed at those outside the church, to prove to them the value of Christianity, but at fellow Christians, to show them the nature of their faith and what true obedience entails. His goal is not respectability, but obedience, and he makes few concessions to the structures and systems of power and prestige around him.

Out of this agenda, there flows a theology that does not seek to view the God of Scripture as an Ineffable One nor as a Supreme Ruler, but as a loving parent, shepherd, and teacher. Nor does Irenaeus seek to enhance the divine majesty by creating a gulf between God and humankind. On the contrary, he envisions a vast divine plan in which humans have a significant role to play—a role which eventually leads to the divinization of even the most humble, in the midst of the new order of a coming Kingdom.

> The Father will excel in wisdom all human and angelic wisdom, because He is Lord, and Judge, and the Just One, and Ruler over all. For He is good, and merciful, and patient, and saves whom He ought: nor does goodness desert Him in the exercise of justice, nor is His wisdom lessened; for He saves those whom He should save, and judges those worthy of judgment. Neither does He show Himself unmercifully just; for His goodness, no doubt, goes on before, and takes precedency.[23]

It is at this point that the powerful, who seek a theology that will endorse their power and the existing order, find it necessary to part company with Irenaeus. A view of human history which promises the divinization of the most humble and a new Kingdom coming from on high will hardly support the notion that the emperor and the present order somehow embody divine purposes. Certainly, the civil order has been instituted by God and should not be questioned—a point Irenaeus under-scores. But he then supplements Romans 13: "Whenever they act in a just and legitimate manner. . . . But whatsoever they do to the subversion of justice, iniquitously, and impiously, and illegally, and tyrannically, in these things shall they also perish."[24] Given the importance of eschatological expectation for Type C theology—an expectation which included peace, love, and justice on earth—it is easy to see why it would not be favored by those in authority.

The reasons Type C theology was generally forgotten after the first few centuries of the history of the church are not purely doctrinal. *Its social and political implications stood in the way of a church and society that wished to make the gospel more acceptable to the established order, and vice versa—the established order more acceptable to the gospel.*

The two other types of theology found a way into Graeco-Roman society by interpreting the Christian faith in terms of the two traditions highly valued by society. Type A uses law and order (first Roman; at later times, Germanic, Napoleonic, etc.) as its point of contact. Type B does the same with philosophy (first Platonic; later, Aristotelian, Cartesian, Hegelian, etc.). All this means that the first two types of theology, even without the knowledge or intention of their exponents, eventually came to serve the interests of the powerful and the intellectual elite. Although at first such people opposed Christianity, which was mocked by the philosophers and persecuted by those who administered the law, after Christianity became the general religion of the Empire, that very elite was content to see it interpreted in terms of law and philosophy.

The general outline of that process will occupy us in the next three chapters.

PART TWO

The Course of Western Theology

*A*FTER *the Empire became Christian, Type C theology was progressively forgotten, while Type A, modified with several elements from Type B, became standard Christian theology, particularly in the West. This modified Type A was dominant throughout the Middle Ages and determined much of the course of medieval theology. At the time of the Reformation, although important issues divided the church, both Protestants and Catholics generally remained within the parameters of that theology. In this respect, traditional Catholic and Protestant theologies are expressions of the same type of theology.*

At various points in the history of Christian thought, those who have felt that Type A—even as modified by the accretion of some elements from Type B—was too confining, have had recourse to various forms of Type B.

Meanwhile, Type C was generally ignored in theological treatises and formulations, though at times a particular emphasis of an individual theologian or movement was reminiscent of it.

VI

Later Patristic Theology: The Role of Augustine

Early in the fourth century, a momentous change occurred in the life of the church: Almost immediately after the greatest of persecutions, it was granted tolerance, and soon Constantine began to grant ever increasing manifestations of his favor. Fifty years later, Christianity was the official religion of the Roman Empire, and steps were being taken to destroy the old pagan religion.[1]

From a certain viewpoint, those changes were unexpected and could be explained by many only as an intervention from on high. That is understandable when one takes into account the enormous sense of relief and vindication felt by those who had lived constantly under the threat or reality of persecution and often had been treated as the worst scum.

On the other hand, looking at it from another perspective and with the hindsight of centuries, one can see that the church had long been unwittingly preparing itself for its new role in Roman society. In a sense, the work of the many Christian apologists, while probably doing very little to avert immediate persecution or to convince the rulers to whom it was often addressed, prepared the way for the post-Constantinian church. Indeed, the apologists had tried to show their enemies—and in fact prove to themselves—that Christianity was not the uncouth, disorderly, radical faith it was said to be.

The case of the apologists who made use of classical philosophy—in fact, the majority of the apologists—is a clear example of this. They set out to show that Christianity was not incompatible with the best of pagan philosophy, and in the end, they and their successors began to use that philosophy as a basic hermeneutical tool to understand the meaning of Scripture and the nature of Christianity.

The same is true, although in a more hidden fashion, of apologists such as Tatian and Tertullian, though the latter has been described as the prototype of the extreme opposition between Christianity and culture. Tertullian had some very harsh words to say about pagan philosophy, indeed. However, in his apologetic task he too set out to show that Christianity was not the monster it was said to be. He did this not by interpreting it in terms of the Platonic tradition, as did his counterparts of Type B, but by interpreting it in terms of law—together with philosophy, one of the two great traditions of which the Greco-Roman world had reason to be proud.

Thus, just as Type B theology showed that Christianity was ultimately compatible with Greek philosophy, Type A showed the same for Roman law and order.

The comments of Part II will be limited to the Western church. No attempt will be made to discover how the Eastern church fits within the framework of the three types of theology. It would seem that the Eastern church, due to the conservative character of its liturgy, has kept in it a great deal that expresses the more ancient perspective of Type C, but its formal and academic theology has often followed Type B. There may well be a connection between this and the fact that throughout much of its history the Eastern church has often found itself under one form or another of caesaropapism (that is, subject to the authority of secular rulers), and therefore its explicit theology has not expressed the radical elements that persist in its liturgy.

This, however, is not a question we need to pursue here, but is best left for others more versed in the historical development of Eastern theology and its connections with the political circumstances of the Byzantine and Russian empires. We shall consider Eastern theology only in its earliest periods, when Western theology was in constant dialogue with it, and it therefore became part of Western tradition.

Our discussion of the course of Western theology will necessarily have the characteristics of an outline, drawing the major lines and leaving much to be filled in. For more details, I once again direct the reader to *A History of Christian Thought*. In any case, the broad lines of what follows should suffice to prove my point, for as Irenaeus would say, "It is not needful . . . that one should drink up the ocean who wishes to learn that its water is salt."[2]

After Constantine's conversion, and as the Empire and the church became increasingly entwined, there was great pressure in favor of the first two types of theology and against the third. In general, such pressure was neither open nor conscious; but from their own social and economic perspectives, the powerful expected the gospel to be compatible with their power. Even among those who were not powerful, there was a tendency to rejoice in the fact that the Empire was now willing to accept what, until then, had been the faith of a powerless and persecuted minority, even though this entailed a certain reinterpretation of that faith.

The individual most characteristic of that attitude is Eusebius of Caesarea. The famous historian often has been accused of being little more than an adulator of Constantine, but his biography shows that such an interpretation misses the mark.[3] Eusebius had suffered for the faith and remained firm; therefore he should not be accused of lacking courage. Furthermore, some of his most extravagant praise of Constantine was written after the emperor's death, and therefore cannot be considered servile adulation. Eusebius seems to have been a sincere person, a faithful exponent of the views of many Christians who finally saw themselves free of persecution, and for whom the conversion of Constantine appeared as an act of providence. Eusebius is important because in his work we see a faithful picture of what was being thought in many Christian circles after Constantine's conversion.

In his theological outlook, Eusebius was a follower of Origen. The latter spent most of his later years in Caesarea, where he left his library, and where some time later young Eusebius was captivated by the intellectual curiosity of Pamphilus, who introduced him to the work of the Alexandrine master. It was thanks to Origen's library that Eusebius was able to carry out his work as a historian.

Therefore Eusebius, a convinced Origenist, believed that Christianity was a series of immutable and eternal truths, revealed in Jesus but perfectly compatible with what the philosophers had already discovered. For this reason it can be said that Eusebius, in spite of being a historian, did not believe in history—at least, not in history as a continuing process.[4] He did not believe that Christian doctrine could possibly have developed. Part of his purpose was to show that Christians in his time held the beliefs they always had held. We know today that this was a false assumption; but the fact that Eusebius is one of our main sources for ancient Christianity complicates the task of modern historians.

In any case, in the great *Church History* and his other writings, he sought to show, among other things, that the Empire was part of God's plans for the propagation of the gospel, and therefore it was perfectly compatible with Christianity. One should not forget that in Eusebius' time, many pagans thought that the movement of the Empire toward Christianity was a great apostasy against the gods who had made Rome great and that these gods would punish the Empire. Furthermore, there were Christian precedents for Eusebius' task, particularly among those who, along the lines of Type B theology, had held that God gave philosophy to the Gentiles to prepare them for the gospel, just as the Law had been given to Jews. Therefore, Eusebius added that the Empire, too, found its crown in the gospel; that it was for the advent of Christianity that God had created the Empire; and that therefore Constantine's experiment, rather than an apostasy on the part of Rome against its gods, or of the church against hers, was the natural consequence of the full development of both the Empire and the church.

Eusebius interprets the entire period of the persecutions as a great error on the part of the Empire. He leaves the reader with the impression that, had Roman authorities really known the nature of Christianity, they would not have persecuted it. This was not a new idea, for it was part of the apologists' defense of Christianity which they had been proposing since the second century. With Eusebius, the notion that the Empire persecuted Christianity through either a misunderstanding or the depravity of a particular ruler became commonplace in church history. There is a measure of truth in this, particularly in the cases of Nero and Domitian.

However, the fact is that some of the emperors who persecuted Christians were among the wisest rulers of antiquity. Diocletian, for instance, was an able statesman, the only person in his time capable of keeping together an empire that threatened to crumble. Yet it was precisely Diocletian who unleashed the greatest of persecutions. Eusebius tells us that Diocletian was following the advice of Galerius; that is certainly possible. What is unbelievable is that Diocletian would follow Galerius' advice without any further inquiry and without reaching the conclusion that, at least in part, Galerius' enmity toward Christians was justified.

Furthermore, had persecution been the result of misunderstanding, it would be difficult to explain why, as years went by and the Empire learned more about Christianity, persecution became more generalized. Indeed, it is possible to trace a line of increasing understanding of Christianity among emperors and civil officials, which also would be the line of increasing persecution—from Trajan, whose governor, Pliny, tortured Christians to find out what this new faith was all about; to Marcus Aurelius, who wrote some well-informed although unsympathetic lines about Christians; on to Diocletian, by whose time the Empire knew Christianity quite well.

All this indicates that Christians, at least to a degree and without being conscious of it, were a subversive element within the Empire. From the perspective of the Empire, they were one more of a series of societies gathered for various purposes on which the Empire came to look askance, fearing they were divisive or even subversive.[5] Their insistence on a single God, to the detriment of the Roman gods, had enormous political consequences, for it tended to divide an Empire built on the basis of religious syncretism and political eclecticism. It also tacitly denied the assumption that Rome had been made great by her gods and by her fidelity to them, thus questioning all of Roman history and self-understanding.

And the claim that the Lord of the universe was a carpenter from Galilee, who had been condemned to death by the Empire, cast doubt on the Roman justice of which the authorities boasted—even though many Christians tried to relieve this tension by placing the blame on Jews rather than on the Empire. Jesus' teaching regarding the poor must have reached the ears of those in authority. The inclination of many Christians toward pacifism—and their objections to military service on other grounds—undermined the strength of an Empire constantly threatened by "barbarians" at its borders.[6] The Christian hope for a kingdom of God, which would supplant all human kingdoms and bring about true peace and justice, was an implicit criticism of the peace and justice of which the Romans were so proud. Therefore, the officers of the Empire were not entirely mistaken in persecuting Christianity. In short, "The Christian movement was revolutionary not because it had the men and resources to mount a war against the laws of the Roman Empire, but because it created a social group that promoted its own laws and its own patterns of behavior."[7]

From this it would follow that the enmity between Christianity and the Empire could not be easily resolved and that the rapprochement taking place with the conversion of Constantine would require radical changes in Christianity, in the Empire, or in both. Therefore Eusebius was compelled to present things otherwise—to claim that the real reason for persecution in the past was the ignorance of those in authority.

While most modern historians have found it necessary to correct Eusebius' account of early Christianity and the period of persecutions on one point or another, few have cast doubt on his basic interpretation of the persecutions as an unfortunate misunderstanding. This is not surprising, since most historians, while censuring Eusebius for his uncritical spirit vis-à-vis Constantine's government, have avoided interpreting the Christian faith in such a way that it would appear to be too critical about their own society.[8] This is why the notion that persecution was a legal tragedy based on misunderstanding has remained to this day, particularly in the popular understanding of those early centuries.

Eusebius' Origenism, joined with his political outlook, led him to undervalue Type C theology, particularly in terms of its eschatological expectation. Since the book of Revelation was one of the main sources of that expectation, Eusebius sought to undermine its authority.[9] Papias also was given short shrift. Eusebius quoted him only in order to prove that the John who had been the teacher of Polycarp and Papias was not John the apostle. He then went on to comment on Papias' materialistic vision of the Kingdom and to conclude that "he had little understanding."[10] Although he could not completely ignore Irenaeus, Eusebius gave no credence to his eschatology and said little about his theology.

Our historian's rejection of the supposedly too materialistic expectations of Revelation, Papias, and Irenaeus can be explained partly on the basis of his Origenism, with its tendency to undervalue physical reality. However, that would not explain why Eusebius did not show the same aversion when praising the riches with which Constantine adorned Christian churches.[11] Once again, political and social perspectives and interests were clothed in the garb of philosophical and theological doctrine.

It would be easy and comfortable to conclude that Eusebius was a hypocritical opportunist, for thus we would avoid applying the lesson to ourselves. But what has happened is much more subtle and therefore more dangerous. Eusebius has unwittingly become part of a long tradition which has interpreted the Christian faith from the perspective of the powerful, or at least to their liking and benefit. Constantine and his successors offered the church the prestige and power of the state, and in exchange, many in the church mollified their message so that it would not be too offensive to the powerful.

By the time of Eusebius, most of the Eastern wing of the church was increasingly influenced by Origen—at least until his condemnation at the Fifth Ecumenical Council. While few were willing to defend his most extreme positions, most formal theology was deeply influenced by his understanding of the Godhead, drawn more from the Platonist tradition than from

Christian sources. Very few theologians during the time of the great councils opposed this Platonization of Christianity. Most of those who did—Paul of Samosata,[12] Eustathius of Antioch,[13] and those who eventually were dubbed Nestorians[14]—were rejected by the church at large and have been considered heretics ever since. That Platonizing view of God was constantly present in the Trinitarian and Christological controversies which shook the church in the fourth and fifth centuries.

The Arian controversy was, to a degree, a dispute between two different sorts of Origenists,[15] and the great contribution of Athanasius was his return to some of the insights of Type C, to thus undercut the bitter dispute between the two wings of Origenism. As to the Christological controversies, they were inevitable, once Type B theology defined God in terms of radical opposition to all human characteristics, for on that basis, to say that God became human was a logical contradiction—like asking for hot ice cream. The Christological question, complicated by all sorts of political and social interests, led to the first permanent divisions in the church and dragged on in the East for centuries.[16]

While the Western branch of the church accepted the Trinitarian and Christological definitions of the Great Councils, it was never deeply involved in the debates or divided by them. It is usually said that this was due to the more practical bent of the Latin mind, in contrast to the more speculative inclination of the Greek. That explanation, which smacks of racism by implying innate aptitudes and characteristics in various races, does not really explain the situation.

In fact, the West, dominated by Type A theology, was spared deep involvement in matters which sprang from the view of truth and of the Godhead which the East had inherited from Type B. Again, this was not due simply to a theological, or intellectual, or temperamental preference on the part of the West. On the contrary, it was closely bound to the different political situation in the West. The founding of Constantinople was a sign of the eastward shift of the center of the Empire. It also indicated that the emperors would increasingly take on the role of absolute ruler, after the fashion of the East. The Western portion of the Empire, which evolved out of the legal system of the Roman republic, had never granted the emperor the absolute power he claimed in the East. In the West, the emperor was the executor of the law; in the East, he became more and more the representative of the divine[17]—or as Eusebius would say, a "bishop of bishops."

Therefore the Western church had more freedom to object to the dictates of the emperors, while in the East, the emperors constantly tried to become arbiters in theological matters. This in turn contributed an added bitterness to theological controversies in the East, for in order to triumph in such controversies, one simply persuaded the imperial authorities to take one's side. During the fourth century, the presence of the West prevented this tendency from becoming extreme. But by the fifth, when the migrations of the Germanic peoples had wreaked havoc in the West, the East could follow is own course, and intervention of imperial fiat in theological discussions became more and more frequent.

As a result, theological causes, down to the least minutiae, were taken as banners by various political parties, and therefore the East saw the development, not only of the different sorts and shades of so-called Nestorianism and monophysitism, but also of monothelism, monergism, and so on—theological positions that sought to define the relationship between the divine and the human in Christ with increasingly subtle distinctions.[18]

Meanwhile, the West followed its own course. In Trinitarian and Christological matters, it was content to see its ancient formulas, first proposed by Tertullian, win the day and become generally accepted—although with different meanings from those Tertullian had given them.

The course the West followed was to develop its own brand of orthodoxy, one which incorporated a number of elements from Type B into what was at heart a Type A understanding of the gospel. Paramount in this process, although by no means its sole architect, was St. Augustine of Hippo.[19] In him we see the basic perspective of Type A, joined with certain elements of Type B in a manner that would be characteristic of most later Western theology. Therefore, for the purposes of our thesis at this point, it will suffice to show how Augustine combines the various elements of these two types of theology.

The spiritual and intellectual biography of Augustine is well known. Born to a Christian mother and a pagan father, a minor Roman officer in North Africa, Augustine eventually gave up the faith of his mother Monica, largely because he could not make sense of it. Since it was the problem of evil that most troubled him, he was attracted to Manichaeism, which claimed to have a solution to that problem. Eventually, disenchanted with Manichaeism, he came upon some Platonic writings, where he discovered what he took to be a solution to the problem of evil as well as a way of thinking about God and the soul which he found more acceptable than those he had heard in either Christian or Manichaean circles. Thus the great contributions of the Neoplatonists to Augustine's theology are to be found in his doctrines of God, of the soul, and of evil. We shall return to these momentarily.

It has often been pointed out that Augustine's famous conversion in the garden of Milan turned him into a Neoplatonic philosopher more than a Christian theologian, and it was only gradually, as he struggled with the tasks of being a bishop and a teacher in the church, that he depurated his theology of excessive Neoplatonic influences and views—such as a universal world soul, and knowledge as reminiscence from a previous existence.[20]

It has not been sufficiently stressed that there is a connection between Augustine's theology and Monica's brand of Christianity. For all its Neoplatonic garb, Augustine's theology reflects the same basic perspective as that of Tertullian. This does not mean that he is another Tertullian. Indeed, his open admiration for the best of pagan culture, particularly for the Platonists, would have been repugnant to his Carthaginian forerunner. Still, Augustine's basic view of the nature of the gospel and of what it means to be saved was that of Type A theology. We shall return to this after we look at the main elements he borrowed from the Platonic tradition—thereafter the main points at which Type B theology would be present in standard Western orthodoxy.

Augustine had difficulties with the view of God he believed his mother and the church to be holding. He states clearly that it was not the teachings of the church, but his reading of the Neoplatonists, that clarified his understanding of God.[21] For him, God was primarily the Ineffable One of the Platonic tradition. God is not properly called a substance, but only an essence. In God there is no time or space, but past and future are as real as the present. God sees everything at once: real or possible; past, present, or future.

This does not mean that time is unreal. Time is such that creation cannot exist without it. It is within time that history takes place. So much has been said about Augustine's philosophy of history that one would be tempted to see there a residue of Type C theology. Yet, when we take a closer look, we are disappointed. For him, it is not the historical course of events that is important, but the life of the spiritual city of God, whose truth, given once and for all, is beyond history, and whose goal is also beyond history.[22] In the end, the result of the historical process will be for naught. The history of the world has no ultimate significance and no connection with God's final purposes.

Nor does this mean that the end will be just like the beginning, as is the case with Origen's thought. On the contrary, Augustine declared that the end would not be a mere return to Eden.[23] The long process of sin and redemption will take us to an even higher state. Had Adam and Eve not sinned, they would have been transposed to that higher plane without the need for any intervening history.[24] Augustine does not see the necessity, as Irenaeus did, that Adam and Eve grow and be taught in justice through what amounted to a historical process. Also, in the end there will be no more history. Augustine has no place for Irenaeus' hope for eternal growth. His view of heaven, as a result of his Platonic influences, has a tendency to be static—although, in his assertion that in heaven we shall retain the freedom not to sin, he affirms an element of freedom and movement which later theology tended to abandon.

The second point at which Neoplatonism influenced Augustine, and through him all of Western theology, is the doctrine of the soul. The notion that the soul is incorporeal, which most later theology takes for granted, had very few supporters in the Western church before the time of Augustine. In the East, mostly through the influence of the Platonic tradition and Type B theology, that notion had come to be generally held; but when Augustine proposed it in the West, many were horrified. Indeed, they could find no biblical basis for the incorporeality of the soul. And in any case, a long tradition that stemmed from Tertullian and was deeply influenced by Stoicism took for granted that the soul was corporeal. Long after Augustine's death, his theory that the soul was incorporeal was debated amid general opposition.[25] Eventually, as a result of both the growing authority of Augustine himself and the increasing influence of Neoplatonism through other sources imported from the East, the controversy subsided, and it was generally admitted without further debate that the soul is incorporeal.

The third point at which Neoplatonic influence was paramount in Augustine was his understanding of evil. As we have said, the problem of evil was one of the most vexing as he sought to understand his mother's faith and the nature of the world. He eventually found his solution in the teaching of the Neoplatonists—that evil is not an entity, but a deprivation of good. In other words, nothing in itself is evil; every nature, qua nature, is good. But it can be perverted and thus become evil. This perversion is understood basically in terms of an unnatural moving away from the good. Thus, for instance, a monkey is beautiful as a monkey; but for a human being to look like a monkey would not be beautiful. What is good in a monkey is evil in a human—not because in itself it is evil, but because it constitutes a corruption of nature, a moving away from the higher toward the lower.

This in turn implies a hierarchical understanding of reality, which was already present in Neoplatonic thought, and through Augustine and later Neoplatonic influences, soon became normative in Western theology. If evil is a moving away from the One, it follows that, although every created nature in itself is good, some are better than others because they are closer to the One. In terms of understanding human nature, this was joined to the notion—also derived from the Platonic tradition—that the intellectual and psychical life is higher than the material, with dire sociopolitical consequences (which I shall explore in another study).[26]

This understanding was also used later for the claim on the part of ecclesiastical authorities that they were above their civil counterparts, as well as for the entire feudal ordering of society, of which one characteristic was the hierarchical view of the universe and social order. Once again, sociopolitical agendas were hidden in what seemed to be purely intellectual matters.

All this, however, ought not to be understood to mean that Augustine was a follower of Type B theology. When it came to his basic understanding of the gospel, he clearly placed himself within the parameters of Type A. This can be seen in the Pelagian controversy, which was really a debate within the camp of Type A—just as the Arian controversy was a debate among followers of Type B.

Pelagianism was a natural outcome of the legalistic and moralistic penchant of Western theology from before the time of Tertullian. The frequent depiction of Pelagius as affirming that human beings are able to merit heaven without God's grace is incorrect. Pelagius did teach that once a believer had repented and begun moving toward good works, God's grace intervened, granting the repentant sinner forgiveness of sins and strengthening the will in its resolve to do good works. Thus sinners were not expected to erase their own sins, but simply to repent and correct their lives, whereupon God would grant forgiveness. This was very similar to Tertullian's opinion two centuries earlier. From this perspective, Pelagius found the doctrines of predestination and original sin repugnant, for they tended to deny the justice of God—*justice* once again understood in the forensic sense of *retribution*.

Augustine rejected these views. He was convinced of the primacy and priority of grace in redemption. He had a deeper sense of the power of sin than did Pelagius. When speaking of the limits of human freedom under a condition of sin, he approached the sense of subjection found earlier in Irenaeus and other Type C theologians. He did not wish to abandon this insight, but his solution put him squarely within the framework of Type A. As sinners, Augustine declared, we are unable to do good. We do not have freedom *not* to sin. Therefore the Pelagian notion that by our own power we are able to do what is demanded of us—repent and begin correcting our lives—must be discarded. We can be saved only because, even in our sinful state, grace intervenes.

Augustine understood grace as a supernatural power that is infused into human beings, enabling them to do that of which they were not capable before. Grace has the initiative. It operates in us before we either wish or ask it to do so, and then it cooperates with us in good works. In a sense, it is grace that saves us. In another sense, we are saved by the merits of those works we do with the presence and cooperation of grace.

For this reason, both Protestant Reformers and their Catholic opponents in the sixteenth century could quote Augustine in support of their views. Salvation is by grace; but this means that it is by grace that the sinner does the good works necessary for salvation.

Augustine did not break away from the fundamental understanding of Type A theology: that we are debtors to the moral order and that salvation takes place by works—either ours or Christ's—which undo that debt. The Pelagian controversy, to which most Western debates on the way to achieve salvation would repeatedly return, took place within those parameters. At this point, one might add that this perhaps substantiates the claims of Eastern Christians that the question of whether salvation is by grace or by works has not been a source of division in the East because they have an entirely different view of the matter. (Whether or not that is the case is beyond the scope of the present essay.)

In passing, one might add that Augustine's doctrine of predestination, which developed within the context of the Pelagian controversy, shows unmistakable characteristics of the legalism of Type A—particularly when he declares that the number of the predestined is exactly the number needed to fill the ranks of the fallen angels;[27] that some sinners had to be damned in order to show God's concern for justice.[28]

However, this debate had another consequence which would make an even greater impact on later Christian theology and piety. In the course of the confrontation with Pelagianism, Augustine came to the conclusion that pride is the root of all sin, the "sin before sin."[29] Although the sinful character of undue pride had been pointed out before, it was Augustine who put pride at the very heart of his understanding of sin because in many ways this seemed to explain much of his religious pilgrimage—and also because *hubris* played a similar role in much of the Greek tradition from which he drew. He may have been right in pointing to pride as his greatest temptation. However, when this view was raised to the level of a general understanding of sin, it came to mean that all pride is by nature sinful; that Christians ought to be content with the place in society that is their lot. For the oppressed to claim freedom and dignity is an act of pride, and therefore sinful.

Finally, Augustine influenced the course of later theology and ethics by his definition of a just war. In contrast to their earlier counterparts, after the time of Constantine, Christian leaders had to come to grips with the degree to which the power of the state ought to be used in support of the church. This became an urgent question for Augustine, for the church in North Africa was rent by the Donatist schism which had taken a violent bent.

It has been pointed out that the Donatist schism was not a purely theological matter, but that there were racial, political, and social factors involved.[30] North Africa had been made a part of the Roman Empire after the Punic wars; but the older Punic and Berber elements in the population never had been assimilated into the new order.[31] The cities—particularly Carthage—were fairly affluent and controlled the productive trade with Italy. A Latin population in the cities, and those of older stock who had been assimilated into the system, profited from that trade. But the lower urban population and most people in the rural areas lived in a situation of economic dependence and exploitation.

When the Donatist schism broke out, the theological issues involved provided banners for ancient grievances.[32] Eventually, the radical wing of the Donatists, the Circumcellions, was waging what amounted to guerrilla warfare against the state. As usual, from the perspective of those who were part of the system, or at least cherished its peace more than they abhorred its injustices, the acts of the Circumcellions were seen as cruel plunder. The Circumcellions themselves, on the other hand, were convinced that they were fighting for a just cause, even more so since it also was the cause of the church, as the Donatists saw it.

At first Augustine and the leaders of that portion of the North African church which preserved its communion with the church at large recommended a rational approach. No one ought to be compelled to come into the church; false Catholics would be the result of such procedures. True Catholics should persuade the Donatists of the error of their ways. This was a sincere wish on the part of Augustine. Peace was to be preserved by an appeal to reason and dialogue. The problem was that what appeared reasonable to Augustine and the anti-Donatist party appeared as sheer continuation of injustice and exploitation to the Circumcellions. Thus the very appeal to reason was unreasonable, and violence against the system and the church—which was increasingly part of it—continued.

Eventually, much against his will, Augustine moved to a position that encouraged the use of force by the state. There can be such a thing as a "just" war. This would be a war that would abide by certain rules, both in the inner attitude involved and in the outer way it would be conducted. The inner attitude should be one of love, in spite of the strife. Outwardly, a just war must avoid plunder, unnecessary death, profanation of churches, and so on. Above all, it should be marked by two characteristics, and these gave Augustine's theory of a just war its conservative bent.

First, a just war must be waged in order to seek peace. No one would argue against that. What is remarkable is that Augustine—and those who developed his theories on this point—did not see the very important fact that a *just* war must, above all, seek *justice*. If peace is understood as the status quo, a war that merely seeks peace can be very unjust. This was the Circumcellions' point, which Augustine, in his commitment to the peace the Empire provided, could not see. (It is ironic that, partly as a result of the failure of the Empire to understand the grievances of the people of North Africa, those people offered little resistance to the Germanic invaders, so that even as Augustine was dying, the Vandals were at the very gates of Hippo. For the same reason, centuries later North Africa offered little resistance to the invading Arabs.)

The second characteristic of a just war, closely related to the first, is that it must be waged by the ruler. In saying this, Augustine was trying to both undercut the Circumcellions and prevent private vengeance and sedition. Yet in fact he was saying—at least as later generations understood it—that rulers may be justified in using violence to suppress those who revolt against them and their understanding of peace, but that those under them, no matter how oppressed, are never justified in taking arms against their rulers. Thus in short, peace and justice are to be defined by those in power. We see in all this some consequences of a theology with the basic perspective of law and order—that is, Type A theology.

Augustine was the great mentor of Western theology, although on one item—his understanding of grace and predestination—his views were never generally held by others. But here too all medieval theologians considered themselves followers of Augustine—as they understood him. In general, however, his combination of what was essentially a Type A theology with elements borrowed from Type B, particularly on the doctrines of God and the soul, became normative for the Middle Ages. During that period, when the church took upon itself the task of preserving law and order, Augustine's understanding of a hierarchical order—strengthened with contributions from other sources—and such items as the just war would prove very useful. Above all, Augustine had given his seal of approval to a concept of the gospel which linked it very closely with the theology of Type A, and which would be dominant throughout the Middle Ages.

VII

Medieval Theology

When Augustine died, the Vandals were practically at the gates of Hippo. Two decades earlier, the Goths had conquered and sacked Rome. There ensued a time of uncertainty, when much of the old *pax romana* broke down, and the church came to play an increasingly active role in the ordering of society. For that role a Type A theology, with its emphasis on law and moral order, was particularly valuable. While significant elements of Type C had appeared in the works of some of the Western "Fathers" of the fourth century, by the time of Gregory the Great (bishop of Rome from 590 to 604), Type A had become dominant.

Gregory considered himself a disciple and exponent of Augustine's theology,[1] and it was through him that the Middle Ages interpreted the teachings of that great bishop of Hippo. There was, however, a vast difference between their times and circumstances. Augustine had lived in a fairly stable world, where he had been able to devote himself to the "philosophical life" until he was forced to become a minister of the church. Even then his administrative responsibilities were limited to Hippo, where the main source of turmoil originated with the more radical Circumcellions, whose depredations were generally limited to relatively remote areas.

Gregory, however, found himself charged with the responsibility of assuring the food and water supply for the city of Rome at a time when those supplies were constantly threatened. Furthermore, his administrative responsibilities included an ever increasing area, as the church was forced to fill the vacuum left by the collapse of the Empire. Therefore order and authority, and the fear of their breakdown, were Gregory's paramount concerns. In a time when there was a constant threat of chaos, the notion that the universe is a moral order and that the gospel is basically a guide for dealing with that order was particularly attractive. This is reflected in Gregory's theology, an adaptation of Augustine's theology to the new times, in which the mood and perspectives of Type A are much stronger than in Augustine's. After Gregory, medieval theology took for granted that only Type A theology was orthodox, that this was what had been held by Christian teachers from the very beginning of the church.

To illustrate the manner in which the Middle Ages followed the fundamental lines of Type A, it will suffice to outline two closely related themes central to the development of medieval theology and piety: the penitential system and the notion of Christ's death as satisfaction for sins.

The penitential system evolved mainly from the question of postbaptismal sins. As we have seen, that question preoccupied Western theologians as early as the middle of the second century, for it can be found in two writings among Tertullian's forerunners: the *Shepherd* of Hermas, and the so-called *Second Epistle of Clement to the Corinthians*. The entire church needed to deal repeatedly with the fact that baptized Christians continued to sin. In the West, where the notion of sin as a debt cancelled by baptism soon became normative, the issue was much more hotly debated than in the East. It is significant that the main schisms that took place in the West, such as those of Hippolytus,[2] the Novatians,[3] and the Donatists,[4] revolved, at least in part, on disagreements regarding the forgiveness of postbaptismal sins and the restoration of the lapsed.

From a very early date, the Western church responded to this issue through the practice of penance. As Hermas shows, at first such penance was permitted only once. This continued to be the practice of the Western church for a long time. The result was that, just as before many had tended to postpone *baptism* until they were on their deathbeds, or at least until such a time as the sins of youth were behind them, now the fear of prematurely exhausting that last opportunity of forgiveness led many to postpone *penance* until their deathbeds, or at least until old age. Several Western theologians in the early Middle Ages mention that practice with dismay.[5] Other texts show that the practice of a final act of penance at the time of death was becoming increasingly common, first in Rome, then in Gaul.[6] At that time penance was a solemn and public act similar to baptism, in which the penitent confessed sins before the bishop and the congregation.

This unrepeatable penance produced various difficulties. It left the penitent devoid of the ministry of the church during the long period between the sin and its forgiveness in public penance. Also, since penance was such a solemn act, to be performed only once, it was usually limited to what seemed the most grievous sins, and thus offered no consolation for the numberless Christians whose daily experience was that, even after baptism, they found themselves committing with some frequency what seemed minor sins. For these reasons, another type of penance slowly evolved, probably at first in monasteries where the monks practiced it among themselves. This new form of penance was less solemn and based on private confession, which could be repeated as many times as necessary. It appeared first in Ireland and Great Britain around the sixth century, and from there spread to the rest of Western Christendom; in scarcely two centuries it was widely practiced, often against the wishes of the hierarchy, who insisted on the ancient, more formal penance.[7] That was the origin of the practice of private penance, which subsists to this day in some Western churches, particularly the Roman Catholic.

This in turn posed other needs. When penance was reserved to take place only once, and had to do primarily with the most blatant sins, or in any case with postbaptismal sins as a whole, it was not necessary to establish detailed distinctions between various sorts of sin in order to impose adequate works of satisfaction. However, now that penance was practiced with certain regularity, people were confessing sins whose gravity seemed to vary. It did not seem just, particularly within the framework of Type A theology, to require the same works of satisfaction from a murderer as from a liar. And even in the case of a liar, one had to take into account the circumstances and the intention with which the sin had been committed. There seemed to be a vast difference between a lie with a good intention, to prevent someone from suffering undue pain, and a lie for one's own benefit.

From that situation sprang an entire body of literature, the "penitential books," the purpose of which was to serve as a guide for the priest in the practice of confession and the determination of penalty. Such books describe and classify all sorts of sin in such minute detail that they often are an excellent description of the life of the times.[8]

Although it became relatively common in the early centuries of the Middle Ages, the practice of private penance was not recognized as a sacrament until much later. It was the Fourth Lateran Council in 1215 that first legislated regarding the obligation of the faithful to avail themselves of this rite.[9] The penitential books then became much more common, and their psychological insight much deeper.[10]

Since within the framework of Type A theology the legal order is of great importance, a distinction was made between the forgiveness granted at baptism and that obtained through penance. While the first was freely given, the later required that sinners offer satisfaction. Therefore, the determination of ecclesiastical penalties soon became one of the main pastoral duties of those in charge of the administration of penance. In theory, the penitent was to undergo a penalty that would merit the forgiveness of the sin confessed.

However, once the question of the forgiveness of sin is thus posed, other difficulties appear. There are those who die without having been able to offer satisfaction for all their sins. Such sins may not be "mortal," but simply "venial"—since a consequence of the Type A approach is that one must classify sins, like crimes, according to their gravity. In any case, those people were not impenitent Christians, but people who, even having had the intention to fulfill their works of satisfaction, die without the opportunity to do so. The doctrine of purgatory developed partly as an answer to that difficulty.

The second difficulty is that, even is a person wishes to offer satisfaction for all the sins committed, such a thing is often impossible. There are many sins, and one continues to commit new ones just as one is seeking to expiate for the old. This difficulty gave rise to the doctrine of the treasury of merits. Let us turn to these two elements in order.

The doctrine of purgatory, as it appears in Western Christianity, is typical of Type A theology. Although Origen did speak of a "purifying fire," he did not mean what later Western theologians understood by purgatory. The Alexandrine meant that there is no such thing as an everlasting hell; that biblical references which seem to point to it really refer to the purification through which fallen spirits must go before they can return to the contemplation of the One. That notion fits perfectly within Origen's system and is quite different from the Western doctrine of purgatory.

The Western view is based on the perspective of Type A, in which the main category is law and the moral order. Within that context, sin is a debt which we owe before God. Baptism washes away all previous sins—and only those. Sins committed after baptism can be forgiven only through penance and the works of satisfaction determined within that context. Given such presuppositions, the question of the final destiny of sincere Christians who die without having made complete satisfaction for all their sins becomes one of paramount importance. To say that they are eternally condemned would imply that very few believers are saved. To say, on the other hand, that they go directly to eternal glory would imply that satisfaction for sin is not really required. It was thus necessary to posit a place where one suffers punishment for sins for which no satisfaction has been made, and to claim that such punishment is not eternal, but temporal. Purgatory is such a place. That doctrine, hesitantly suggested by Augustine,[11] and categorically affirmed by Gregory the Great,[12] gained in popularity until the Second Council of Lyon, in 1274, made it a dogma of the church.[13]

The other doctrine that grows out of this theological perspective is the treasury of merits. If salvation is seen as a process through which we cancel our debt with God, as is characteristic of Type A theology, merits become particularly important. Without them, it is impossible to be saved, except in the extremely rare case of one who dies immediately after baptism without having committed any sin after receiving that rite—and even such a person is saved by the merits of Christ.

It is clear that many Christians, in spite of their sincerity and good intentions, are not able to offer sufficient satisfaction for all their sins. It is at this point that it becomes important that the church have a treasury of merits, gained by the saints and by Jesus. According to that doctrine, which took its classical form in the thirteenth century and was held by all orthodox scholastic theologians thereafter, the church has the management of that treasury and can apply its benefits to those Christians whose individual works of satisfaction are insufficient.

Although such a view seems rather crude, one should not forget the important pastoral role it plays within the framework of Type A theology. On its basis, the average Christian, who is far from being a saint but who believes that salvation is attained by undoing the debt of sin, can still hope to be saved. It also should be noted that the treasury of merits allowed this type of theology to apply the merits of Christ to the life of believers after their baptism, thus partly correcting one of the major shortcomings of Type A as compared with Type C.

The treasury of merits was intimately connected with the question of indulgences. These were not originally decreed or defined by ecclesiastical authority, but rather developed out of the practice of penance, having in the background the image of God as legislator or judge, and of sin as a debt owed to the divine order. In the period from the seventh to the tenth centuries, while private penance was becoming increasingly common, confessors often found themselves in situations where the penitent, for various reasons, was unable to offer the prescribed satisfaction. In such cases, pastors would substitute a more adequate penalty. Somewhat later, by joining that use to the theory of the treasury of merits, increasingly radical substitutions were made—for instance, if one could not go on pilgrimage, one could cover the expenses for someone to go in one's stead. It seems that this practice first gained widespread acceptance in Ireland, from there passed to Great Britain, and on to the Continent in the eighth and ninth centuries.

By the end of the ninth century, one of the main concerns of penitential books was the setting of guidelines for such commutations. That trend continued to the point that Urban II, in proclaiming the First Crusade, offered "plenary indulgence" to those who would respond to his call. All penalties the crusaders owed for their sins would be commuted if they would go to the Holy Land to fight the infidel. In 1300, Boniface VIII offered plenary indulgence to all pilgrims who went to Rome in celebration of that year's jubilee.

By then, indulgences had lost a great deal of their original character as a commutation and were seen more as an absolution, which the church could grant on the basis of its treasury of merits.[14] From then on, indulgences were granted in exchange for gifts, and this eventually led to the practice of selling them, against which the Reformers would protest in the sixteenth century. Thus, the dominance of Type A theology in the West would have far-reaching consequences for the development of the penitential system, and for the entire history of Western Christianity.

The celebration of communion became another means whereby Western Christianity attempted to offer satisfaction for sin. The church had held, since its earliest times, that there existed a close relationship between communion and salvation. However, the earliest Christian theologians never claimed that communion gave merit—particularly since the very notion of merit would have been so foreign to Type C theology, which was then dominant— and preferred to speak of it as the means whereby, in being united to Christ and fed by him, we partake of his life.

During the Middle Ages it became customary to speak of the Eucharist as a repetition of Christ's sacrifice, by virtue of which the merits of that sacrifice could be applied both to those present and to others, including the dead. That notion, which appears in the writings of Gregory the Great,[15] became the basis for the celebration of masses for the dead, which has continued to be a practice of the Roman Catholic Church through the centuries.

Since the work of Christ now centered exclusively on the cross, where he made expiation for the sins of humankind, the communion service, which at first had been a celebration of the

resurrection and the coming Kingdom, now took on increasingly funereal overtones. While it was still normally celebrated
on Sunday—the day of the resurrection—the mood was more
appropriate for Friday—the day of the crucifixion.

Throughout this chapter, we have repeatedly spoken of
satisfaction, one of the characteristic themes of Type A theology.
The first to use this term within the context of penance was
Tertullian,[16] and ever since, "satisfaction" has been one of the
characteristic themes of Western theology when dealing with sin
and forgiveness.

Although Tertullian does not speak of the work of Christ as a
satisfaction, that notion appears in the fourth century in
Ambrose of Milan,[17] and in Hilary of Poitiers,[18] and became the
typical way in which Western theologians have spoken of
redemption. Jesus has offered for us the satisfaction which
otherwise we would be required to offer, but of which we are
incapable.

This understanding of the work of Christ as a vicarious
satisfaction for the sins of humankind found its classical
expression in Anselm of Canterbury. This is the main point of
his treatise *Why God Human?* in which he speaks of the
"satisfaction which can only be given by God, which should only
be given by a human, and which must be given by a God
human."[19] According to him, the degree of an offense depends
on the offended, and that of an honor depends on the one who
offers it. This was a principle of Germanic law which Anselm
adapted to theological discussion—another instance of Type A
theology interpreting the gospel in the light of the social order of
the time. From that principle, it follows that sin, as an offense
against God, is infinite.[20] This infinitude has nothing to do with
the act itself, but is measured by the majesty of God, which has
been offended. In other words, any sin, even the most seemingly
minor, is infinite, for it is committed against the supreme divine
majesty.

On the other hand, any satisfaction humans can offer is
measured by the one who offers it, and no finite human being
can offer God satisfaction for sin, since sin is infinite and humans
are finite. Furthermore, since we already owe God all the good

we are able to do—notice once again the language of debt and duty—we can never repay for past sins. How, then, can humankind offer satisfaction to God?

Anselm's answer is well known: Since satisfaction must be offered by humankind, and since it must be infinite, the only possible solution is an infinite human being, and that is the reason for the incarnation. As a human being, Jesus offered God a human satisfaction; as divine, he offered an infinite satisfaction.

With minor changes, this way of understanding the work of Christ has become so common in Western theology that both Catholics and Protestants often believe that this is the only doctrine of redemption, or the one that is most faithful to the Bible.

The fact is that such a doctrine did not appear in the history of Christian thought until a relatively recent date, and even then it was not accepted without opposition. In Type B theology, Jesus is above all the teacher, example, and illuminator. In Type C, he is the conqueror of the powers of evil, the liberator who opens new possibilities. It is significant that even among Type A theologians, the interpretation of the work of Christ as satisfaction took a long time to become generally accepted, for the most commonly held view still saw Jesus as victor and liberator. However, there is no doubt that the theory of vicarious satisfaction fits perfectly within the framework of Type A, and therefore, sooner or later it was bound to appear.

Not all Western theologians during the Middle Ages agreed with the manner in which Type A theology was becoming dominant. Many, usually scholars, found it excessively legalistic and rigid, as well as unenlightened. At this point, it is remarkable that when such opposition arose, it had recourse to Type B, not to Type C, which was generally ignored. In order to illustrate that phenomenon, a brief word about two reactions to Type A orthodoxy should suffice. These reactions are those of John Scotus Erigena and Peter Abelard, both of whom took the option offered by Type B, although in widely differing forms, and they serve to illustrate the evolution of that type of theology during the Middle Ages.

Erigena was a native of Ireland,[21] at that time an intellectual center which kept alive a great deal of the knowledge and scholarship of Greek and Christian antiquities lost to the rest of Western Christendom. Erigena went to the Frankish kingdom toward the middle of the ninth century, probably at the invitation of Charles the Bald. There he translated into Latin several Greek writings, including those of Pseudo-Dionysius, and became famous for his scholarship, although very few—if any—were willing to accept all his teachings.

It could be said that Erigena was the Origen of the ninth century, since his theology, a vast system, found its inspiration in the Platonic tradition. He carried Type B to its ultimate consequences, going so far as to affirm that the Bible had been written for the simpleminded; it was for that reason that it spoke in metaphors.[22] The wise know that the Bible really speaks of higher realities. Thus, for instance, the Scripture passages about God's love, mercy, and wrath are no more than a series of metaphors. In reality, God is ineffable, for the divine reality is beyond any human conception or description.

In Erigena's main work, *On the Division of Nature,* he asserts that nature—that is, all reality—appears in four modalities: creating and uncreated nature, which is God; creating and created nature, the ideas or primordial causes of the Platonic tradition; uncreating created nature, which we usually call creation; and uncreating uncreated nature, simply another way of speaking about God—not now as Creator, but rather as the final goal of all reality.

According to Erigena, the world is made "out of nothing"— not that it has been made out of a vacuum, but that it has been made out of God, whose existence is so beyond all human language and thought that it can properly be called "nothing." Therefore creation was made not only *by* God, but also *from* God. That theory, very close to pantheism, was one of the reasons Erigena had few followers, and why his theology was eventually condemned.

The third level of nature, the one we normally call creation, in truth is purely spiritual. All beings are incorporeal, for bodies are simply constellations of incorporeal realities. Furthermore, in the end all creation will return to God, its origin and end. As to hell, is it only a metaphor which refers to the sufferings that take place in a sinner's conscience.

Although in later centuries Erigena's works were read and quoted with relative frequency, he had no followers. His doctrines and theories, which point to a great intellect, were too distant from what was held by the church at that time—or at any time. On this point, too, he resembled Origen, who also had many readers and partial followers, but few disciples. In any case, Erigena's system stands as an example of protest against the rigid legalism of Type A theology and serves to illustrate our present thesis—that when Western theologians have sought for an alternative to Type A, they usually have followed the option offered by Type B.

Interestingly enough, Erigena's greatest influence on Christian theology in later centuries was not a result of his own works, but of his translation of the works of Pseudo-Dionysius.[23] These writings, said to have been penned by Dionysius, the disciple of Paul, were in fact the product of a much later age, deeply influenced by Neoplatonism and its form of mysticism. Following the Neoplatonic scheme, their view of the universe and the church was strictly hierarchical. It is significant that Western theologians, believing that this was the work of a direct disciple of Paul, gave it great authority, but read it from the perspective of Type A theology. Thus the most significant contribution of Pseudo-Dionysius to Western medieval theology was his hierarchical view of reality, which was used to undergird the hierarchical structures of society and of the church.

In a way, the driving force of Abelard's thought was similar to Erigena's. He too was dissatisfied with the theology of his time; he too offered an alternative that followed the basic lines of Type B, although its contents were very different from both Origen's and Erigena's. Abelard, best known in later times for his romance with Heloise, was famous during his lifetime for his intellectual acuity. He seems to have enjoyed showing up the shortcomings of his teachers, some of whom eventually enjoyed their revenge. For him, there was no human faculty higher than reason, and therefore he devoted himself to the cultivation of it.

The net result was that several of the most powerful church leaders of his time accused him of being a heretic, thus contributing to what Abelard called his *History of Calamities.*

Without attempting to expound the totality of Abelard's theology, some elements of it show that it was a reaction to Type A and that in that reaction, he had recourse to Type B.[24]

The first of those elements is his theological method. Like Origen and other exponents of Type B, Abelard attempted to develop a rational theology; he therefore was accused of being excessively rationalistic. In his *Yes and No,* he collected supposedly authoritative sayings from the Bible and early Christian writers to show that, when posed specific questions, those authorities did not agree among themselves. The purpose of this exercise seems to have been to illustrate the need to appeal to reason and logic in order to reconcile such widely diverging words.

Although he lived before the time of the great rediscovery of Aristotelian metaphysics by Western Europe, Abelard had an extraordinary grasp of Aristotelian logic, on the basis of which he repeatedly worsted and shamed his teachers, and also arrived at an answer to the question of universals that was quite compatible with Aristotelian metaphysics. Thus, some who accused him of excessive rationalism were in fact disturbed by the introduction into theology of a different philosophical approach—one that had not yet been brought into the framework of orthodoxy as had Augustinian Platonism.

Second, in dealing with ethics, Abelard opposed the legalism of his times; he emphasized the importance of intention above action and results.

And third, as to the work of Christ, Abelard rejected both Anselm's theory and the more ancient one that Christ is the conqueror of the powers of evil. According to Abelard, Christ offered us an example and teaching, both verbally and in his actions. The Savior's purpose was to enable us to love the Creator once again, by showing us God's love for us. It was not God who stood in need of reconciliation or satisfaction, as Anselm would have us think, but we, who need to be reminded of the divine love. Such a view of the work of Christ, which, after due allowance for the distance of centuries did follow the main lines of the Alexandrines, was not entirely rejected by the church at large—which has always affirmed that Christ is indeed an example and teacher—but was declared to be insufficient. What many found objectionable was that Abelard failed to include the objective value or effectiveness of the work of Christ. One of the main characteristics of Type B theology is precisely this tendency to reduce the work of Christ to that of teacher, example, and illuminator. For this reason, as well as for others, Abelard was condemned by the church of his time.

Some time after his death, medieval scholastics began to employ a method that drew part of its inspiration from Abelard's *Yes and No.* They would pose a question, cite—or invite others to cite—authorities which could be interpreted in opposing ways, and then finally resolve the matter with a solution that both answered the question and responded to the objections cited. Also, with the invasion of the West by Aristotelian writings and philosophy in the thirteenth century, many of the great scholastics came to philosophical positions—for instance, regarding the question of universals—which were very close to Abelard's; some of them also were accused of excessive rationalism.

Even Thomas Aquinas, who eventually became the most influential Western theologian after Augustine, was regarded askance, and several of his positions were condemned before his authority became widely accepted. If eventually he was accepted as a great exponent of orthodoxy, this was possible because he reconciled the new Aristotelian outlook with the modified Type A theology received from Augustine and his successors. Thus, while Thomas introduced a new way of looking at the nature of the universe and the relationship between philosophy and theology, he did not question the traditional Type A; perspective of Western theology.

All this seems to confirm our thesis that medieval theology, except in such areas as its doctrines of God and the soul where Augustine and others had introduced elements from Type B, was dominated by the perspective of Type A; and that those who sought to free themselves from Type A usually had recourse to Type B.

VIII

The Reformation and Beyond

Luther's spiritual pilgrimage is well known,[1] and his great discovery of justification by faith is often hailed as the starting point of the Protestant Reformation. However, when we look at the events of the sixteenth century from the perspective of our typologies, it is clear that to a significant degree the question Luther asked was still posed within the framework of Type A.

Luther's great preoccupation was the forgiveness of sins. His efforts to attain that forgiveness through confession and penance are characteristic of Type A theology's understanding of Christianity. The future Reformer's despair when his efforts did not give him the peace and security he sought is also characteristic. If salvation is based on the cancellation of our debt before God, there is always doubt as to whether our payment is sufficient. It was for this reason that the medieval church had to offer all sort of guarantees, for otherwise Christians would live in a state of constant incertitude and anguish. Indulgences, the treasury of merits, and purgatory were means to assuage that anguish, giving a believer whose works were insufficient the possibility of still attaining salvation. Luther, however, lived in a time when the authority of the church had begun to weaken. It was not that he destroyed that authority, but rather that its erosion forced him to seek the assurance of his salvation elsewhere. A path he followed for a while, and on which many had found an answer to similar problems, was mysticism. It was only after all alternatives failed that Luther took the untrodden way of justification by faith.

It is often said that it was this discovery that gave birth to the Protestant Reformation. To a degree, what Luther discovered was that Type A theology was inadequate for the understanding of Scripture. The gospel does not consist in a new way to pay for

123

our sins. The gospel is, on the contrary, the Good News that we do not need to pay for them, that God declares us to be just, that we are absolved. However, in all this, Luther is still thinking within the framework of Type A. It is still a matter of a God whose decrees have been disobeyed, and of human beings whose great problem is the debt that follows that disobedience. Luther discovered that the debt had been cancelled, yet he continued to pose the question in terms of debt and satisfaction.

On the other hand, Luther's earlier discovery that sin is much more than a debt owed to God gave impetus to his doctrine of justification by faith. His spiritual pilgrimage showed him that sin is a bondage from which human beings cannot be set free by simply willing it. The manner in which Luther speaks of the power of demons over human will reminds us a great deal of Irenaeus' thoughts on the matter.[2] Due to his own experience, Luther believed that the human problem was not so much that we owe a debt to God, as that we are tied to sin and the powers of evil. Therefore, although he began by seeking forgiveness for his sins and the cancellation of his debt before God, in the midst of his struggle he discovered that the problem was much deeper, for it was no less than bondage of the will to the Evil One, to such a point that the human will by itself is unable to be reconciled to God.

This was the basis for Luther's doctrine of predestination, which occasioned his break with Erasmus.[3] The latter was convinced that Christianity was a moral system of reward and punishment, which requires that human beings be free. Luther's doctrine, in which the sinner is a slave to Satan, appeared to Erasmus as a threat to Christian life and the entire moral system. The Reformer, on the other hand, knew that sin is much more than an evil action we choose or an evil thought we harbor. Sin is slavery, and the only way to become free is through the intervention of a power greater than both ourselves and our slavemaster. All this, in spite of the differences resulting from the centuries between Irenaeus and Luther, is characteristic of Type C theology.

The same may be seen in the way Luther sees the work of Christ. Although his writings contain frequent references to the commonly held doctrine that Jesus is a payment for our sin,

Luther did see Jesus as the conqueror who frees us from the powers that held us in bondage.[4]

The manner in which Luther understands the Word of God also leads him back to Type C theology.[5] What he means by "Word of God" is not a book of rules to be obeyed and doctrines to be held, as in Type A, nor a series of symbols and metaphors pointing to eternal and immutable truths, as in Type B. The Word of God is the very God in creative and redemptive action. When God speaks, that word is itself a divine action, as may be seen both in Genesis and in the prologue to the Fourth Gospel: "God said, 'let there be' . . . and there was"; "All things through him (the Word) were made." The Word of God does not merely give information; it is a power that creates new realities. Jesus is the Word of God because in him God speaks and acts; because he is God, acting for our salvation. The Bible is the Word of God—not because it is an infallible legislation or a handbook of philosophical truths, but because in it we meet Jesus Christ, the living Word of God. It is this Word that conquers the power of evil. The Word, therefore, is the liberating action of God.

In his doctrine regarding baptism, Luther also recovers some elements of Type C theology. For the Reformer, baptism is not only the beginning of the Christian life and the washing away of all previous sin, but also a sign under which the totality of the Christian life takes place.[6] The fact of being baptized, like that of being justified, is not something that simply took place in the past, and we are now left to fend for ourselves. Baptism is valid throughout life, for in it we die and are raised with Christ. Those who see the value of baptism only in reference to past sin do not see all its significance. At every step, Christians can overcome the power of evil precisely because they *are* baptized. Baptism, like birth, is good for the whole of life. When Luther was tempted to set aside the promises and forgiveness of God, he would say: "I am baptized." This affirmation helped him overcome his temptation, and therefore baptism was valid not only for the past, but for the present. From this perspective, in sharp contrast with Type A, postbaptismal sins pose no greater problem than those that took place before baptism.

In spite of all this, the Reformer was not able to free himself from Type A theology in his view of history. Luther saw history as the result of sin. God did not intend for Adam and Eve to remain forever as they were created, but intended to translate them to heaven. Had there been no sin, this would have been done directly, without the intervention of history.[7] At this point, Luther differs radically from Irenaeus.

In his overriding emphasis on justification,[8] Luther also remains within the framework of Type A theology. He is concerned only with whether we are reconciled with God. About the implications of that reconciliation, or about the growth God plans for human beings, he has little to say.

The joining of these two elements produces what traditionally has been the weakest point in Lutheran theology—its inability to deal effectively with the historical matters of the political world. Even in its kindest interpretation, Luther's doctrine of the Two Kingdoms turns the state into little more than a remedy for or a limit to human sin.[9] This in turn means that not many of his theological criteria can be applied to Christians' participation in political life. The "justice" of God is "the passive righteousness {or justice} with which merciful God justifies us by faith."[10] Through such reductionism, much of what Scripture says about a God who requires justice in human relations is lost.

For this reason, it is not surprising that churches within the Lutheran tradition have found it difficult to face concrete problems of politics and justice in their countries.[11] Luther's own interventions in political matters were usually disastrous, as in the cases of the Peasants' War and the bigamy of Philip of Hesse. Lacking a view that saw an ultimate significance in history, Luther was forced to judge all situations on the basis of his main concern for the gospel as the doctrine of reconciliation by faith.

Luther's partial rediscovery of Type C theology was less noticeable in the other major Reformers. Zwingli,[12] with his humanist and philosophical interests, leaned toward Type B theology, particularly in his doctrine of predestination, which he expounded not as the result of the overwhelming experience of God's unmerited grace, but as the necessary corollary to divine omnipotence and omniscience. Also, like the earlier Type B theologians, Zwingli interpreted the significance of the sacraments in largely symbolic terms.

Calvin paid more attention than did Luther to the state and to political relations, and his interest in sanctification led him beyond the overriding emphasis on justification characteristic of Lutheran theology.[13]

However, his fundamental vision was a return to many elements of Type A theology which Luther had abandoned—one should not forget that Calvin's early education had been that of a lawyer. The most notable of these elements is the understanding of the work of Christ as a satisfaction for our sins. Without rejecting that theory, Luther had underscored the victory of Christ over sin and the powers of evil, but Calvin returned to the Anselmian theory.[14] So while Zwingli leaned toward Type B, Calvin tended to retain type A.[15]

The Anabaptist tradition deserves special consideration in this context.[16] Although many details of their doctrine kept the traditional views of type A, some leaders did rediscover the historical dimension of the biblical message. It was partly this that led them to a vivid eschatological expectation of a Kingdom of justice, where the poor would receive their due. It is significant that in the sixteenth century the theme of the New Jerusalem runs through the various branches of radical Anabaptism.[17] Their more radical branch has been criticized by more conservative elements on the basis of such experiments as the one at Münster, where Anabaptists took power and established an increasingly eccentric theocracy. Yet there is no doubt that these radical Anabaptists had rediscovered an element in the biblical message which had been forgotten or simply laid aside by most others. Again, this should not be seen apart from the social and political agendas of the time. Perhaps many Anabaptists were able to see the biblical demand for social justice precisely because they themselves were suffering great injustice. And perhaps Lutherans, Reformed, and Roman Catholic leaders were unable to see this because they were inflicting the injustice—or were supported by the system inflicting it.

Later generations, Lutheran as well as Reformed, lost many of the elements of Type C which Luther—and to a lesser degree, Calvin—had rediscovered. Lutheran,[18] as well as the Calvinist,[19] orthodoxy placed the great Protestant themes (authority of Scripture, justification by faith, divine initiative in salvation) within a Type A scheme, although they frequently included the same elements from Type B that medieval theology had accepted—those having to do with God and the soul. Protestant orthodoxy saw the Bible as the Word of God because it was infallible and provided correct information regarding Christian doctrine.[20] Thus Luther's understanding of the Word of God as creating and liberating was lost. The name of Protestant Scholasticism was justly deserved—not only because its methodology was similar to that of the medieval scholastics, but because in its basic outline it followed the lead of Type A theology, which had been dominant during their time.

In response to the Protestant orthodoxy of the seventeenth and eighteenth centuries, and to an equally rigid Roman Catholicism, two different reactions took place: Rationalism and Pietism. Both these movements, in many ways opposed to each other, bewailed the rigidity of orthodoxy and sought other alternatives.

Rationalism, like Erigena and Abelard in other centuries, sought refuge in Type B theology. For Rationalism, it was important to discover eternal truths—those that never change, that are not subject to human frailty. It is not mere coincidence that Descartes decided to apply the mathematical method to his search for such truth.[21] Mathematical truths, like the Ineffable One of the Platonists, never change. This is why both are universal and indubitable. In the same tradition, both Spinoza and Leibniz were mathematician turned philosopher.[22] The way all these philosophers understood God, as well as all other realities, clearly places them within the tradition of Type B.

Rationalism followed a somewhat different course in Great Britain: instead of taking the idealist path of Cartesianism, it followed Locke's empiricism.[23] When it eventually led to Deism,[24] this philosophical tradition affirmed the truth of "natural religion"—the doctrines of the existence of a Supreme Being, the immortality of the soul, and reward and punishment after death. Anything that went beyond this and claimed to be based on revelation was seen by the Deists as sheer superstition. They were willing to accept any Christian doctrine that could show itself to be based on universal reason, not on a historical revelation given in a concrete place to a particular people. In other words, they felt that truth was to be found in the universal data which natural reason can discover, not in historical events. We have here another case in which a reaction against the rigidity of Type A theology led to Type B, with the result that the historical elements of Christianity—and of Judaism—were shunted aside or denied.[25]

The other reaction to the rigidity of Protestant orthodoxy (as well as against the intellectualism of Rationalism) was Pietism.[26] This movement, which developed mostly in Germany among Lutherans, insisted that the Christian faith involved more than the detailed doctrines of Protestant Scholasticism or the natural religion of the Rationalists. Within Pietism, there was a renewed understanding of worship as an occasion for union with Jesus Christ, and in this may be found an element of Type C. However, in its insistence on individual faith to the detriment of a biblical view of history, and particularly in the tendency of later generations to turn "piety" into a series of rules of conduct, Pietism remained within the realm of Type A theology.

In England, with the Wesleyan movement,[27] Pietism took a somewhat different form. Wesley's conservative political stance —with the notable exception of his opposition to slavery—prevented him from underscoring the historical dimensions of the gospel, which he continued to interpret, in typical Type A fashion, as the means of attaining salvation through the grace of God, who has paid for our sins in the cross of Christ.

However, in contrast to German Pietism, which developed within a Lutheran framework, Wesleyanism took shape within a Calvinist context. Except on the issues raised during the previous century by the Arminian controversy,[28] Wesley was a Calvinist. Therefore Wesley and his followers were not content with affirming the doctrine and experience of justification, as the Pietists had done on the Continent, but insisted also on sanctification. For Wesley himself, and afterward, for the entire movement, that sanctification took on a social and collective character well beyond the purely individual,[29] and thus approached the vision of Type C theology. It should also be remembered that Wesley was a patristic scholar and that in his studies of early Christian theology, he discovered insights that had long been forgotten. In spite of all this, there always has been a faction within its various branches that has sought to reinterpret Methodism along the lines of Continental Pietism, emphasizing justification over sanctification, or personal sanctification over what Wesley would call "social" sanctification.

During the nineteenth century, history became a major concern of theologians and philosophers. In order to understand this emphasis, one must go back as far as the thirteenth century and the reintroduction of Aristotle into western Europe. Until that time, the Platonic understanding of knowledge, modified by Augustine into a theory of knowledge as illumination, had been dominant in Christian thought. The senses and their perception had little to do with true knowledge, and therefore what the senses can perceive, either natural or historical, is of limited permanent value, and the wise should not spend time studying such matters.

But the reintroduction of Aristotle in the thirteenth century brought western Europe into contact with a theory of knowledge in which the senses played an important role. It is no coincidence that Albert the Great, Thomas's teacher, wrote not only on theological and philosophical matters, but also on the natural sciences. From that point, Western civilization became increasingly aware of the significance of the material and temporal world. The rapid development of science and technology begun during the Renaissance made people aware that new things do indeed take place in time and that therefore history is much more than a meaningless narrative of essentially similar events.

By the nineteenth century, the idea of history had so captivated the Western mind that Hegel proposed a system of philosophy in which history was central.[30] Although Hegel, being an idealist, still considered history to be the unfolding of thought in the universal mind, soon others moved beyond him and began to study history as the arena in which significant reality takes place. Karl Marx, basing much of his thought on Hegel's philosophy, developed a view of history and its culmination with a structure very similar to that of ancient Jewish and Christian apocalypticism. (It should be remembered that Marx himself was a Jew.) Darwin's theory of evolution, much debated today for other reasons, may be seen as an extension of the idea of history beyond human events, to the entire biological order.

In theological studies, the idea of history made its impact in the appearance of historical and critical methods for the study of the Bible in the work of scholars such as F. C. Baur and D. F. Strauss; in the development of the discipline of the "history of dogmas," the basic presupposition of which is that dogmas do indeed change and reflect their various historical circumstances; and in the work of J.F.W. Bossuet, Ernst Troeltsch, and the entire *Religionsgeschichtliche Schule*.[31]

Partly as a result of such historical inquiry, many scholars became convinced that the rigid stance of traditional theology —Type A theology—was no longer tenable, and they therefore turned to liberalism. Liberalism is not an unavoidable consequence of the historical study of the Bible, but it does become attractive when such study takes place within the static framework of Type B theology. Since historical research, as well as the pressure of "modern" times, made it impossible for liberal theologians to continue to affirm Type A's understanding of the Bible, they turned to Type B. They then sought, within the historical process of Scripture, the eternal, universal, and immutable truths.

While liberal theologians did not agree on what those truths were, they did agree that indeed there are such truths and that in them was the essence of Christianity. Albrecht Ritschl sought those perennial truths in the moral teachings and example of Jesus.[32] Troeltsch spoke of a "religious *a priori*." By the end of the century, Adolf Harnack could summarize the teachings of Jesus under three headings: "Firstly, the kingdom of God and its coming. Secondly, God the Father and the infinite value of the human soul. Thirdly, the higher righteousness and the commandment of love."[33]

And lest anyone be led to believe that we ought to revive the eschatological expectations of the early church, Harnack clarified his meaning:

> If anyone wants to know what the kingdom of God and the coming of it meant in Jesus' message, he must read and study his parables. He will then see what it is that is meant. The kingdom of God comes by coming to the individual, by entering into his soul and laying hold of it. True, the kingdom of God is the rule of God; but it is the rule of the holy God in the hearts of individuals; *it is God himself in his power*. From this point of view everything that is dramatic in the external and historical sense has vanished; and gone, too, are all the external hopes for the future. . . . It is not a question of angels and devils, thrones and principalities, but of God and the soul, the soul and its God.[34]

In making such assertions, Harnack—as well as many before and after him—claimed to be speaking for the "modern" person. It is interesting to note that during the very century in which liberalism flourished, Christianity rapidly gained converts throughout the world, and many of those converts would have found Harnack's view of Christianity—and of "modernity"—quite surprising.

This points to the main weakness in this theology. As in every other theology of Type B, it is the notion that the theologians themselves have of the eternal truths that becomes the ultimate criterion—even above the biblical text. Therefore it is not surprising that most liberal theologians reached conclusions very similar to those of the liberal philosophers and politicians of their time. In fact, a close relationship existed between theological liberalism and political liberalism, for just as the latter was the social expression of the values and interests of the bourgeoisie, the former was its religious expression.

At this point it may be necessary to clarify the meaning of *liberal*, which has become muddled in the more recent use of the word in political circles in the United States. In its original meaning, economic and political liberalism was the position of those who believed that free enterprise and free competition, with as little state intervention as possible, was the ideal economic order, one that would bring prosperity to the entire world—the doctrine of laissez faire—the position that now in the United States is called "conservative"! This view was held by the rising capitalist class, which often was convinced that the emerging economic order was best—not only for them, but for all—and soon these views pervaded not only the circles of those who controlled the capital, but also the academic and ecclesiastical circles.

Theological liberalism was the counterpart of political and economic liberalism. Both agreed that an elite—be it economic or intellectual—knew what was best for the rest and had a clearer understanding of the workings of society and the meaning of the gospel (an elitist attitude very similar to that of the Alexandrine theologians, who were convinced that the deeper truths of the gospel could be reached only by the enlightened). Therefore, we should not be surprised that liberal theologians often understood the gospel in terms that were entirely compatible with the attitudes and goals of the rising bourgeoisie.[35]

The one point at which theological liberalism seemed for a moment to transcend the limits of its social origins was the Social Gospel movement under the leadership of Rauschenbusch. In Rauschenbusch's theology, one can find an understanding of the power of organized evil rare among theologians of his time, for whom the notion of such a power would have brought the theory of laissez faire into question. Rauschenbusch's experiences in the area of New York known as Hell's Kitchen led him to a deeper understanding of the underside of laissez-faire economics and to a vision of the kingdom of God in its dimensions of social justice. In this he recovered a fundamental biblical theme which had been forgotten in much traditional theology: "They {the early Christians} hoped for a change complete and thorough; for an overturning swift and catastrophic; for an absolute transition of power from those who now rule to those who now suffer and are oppressed. What else is a revolution?"[36]

Unfortunately, later generations in the Social Gospel movement were carried away by other impulses within the liberal tradition, and thus came to a naive understanding of the powers of evil and to the bourgeois understanding of the kingdom of God which Rauschenbusch himself had rejected.

Liberalism provoked strong reactions. The most important within Protestant theology was fundamentalism, essentially a reaffirmation of type A theology. It is significant that when a group of conservatives gathered at Niagara Falls in 1895 and issued the list of five "fundamentals" that would give fundamentalism its name, two of those were characteristic of Type A theology: the inerrancy of Scripture; and the substitutionary death of Jesus (interpreted here in terms of payment for our sins[37]). The other three—the virgin birth, the physical resurrection of Jesus, and his impending return—were included mostly because they were denied by many liberals; they were used as touchstones for the inerrancy of Scripture, rather than as points of particular theological significance.

The virgin birth, in a rather impoverished understanding, was reduced to a biological theory to explain how Jesus could be both divine and human. The resurrection was also impoverished by reducing it to proof that Jesus was divine and that we too will be raised. The return of Jesus was usually divorced from the dimensions of justice in the Kingdom. Thus, while claiming to be a return to biblical faith, fundamentalism in fact impoverished that faith by reducing it—as Type A so often does—to a series of rules of action and belief.

Similar developments were taking place within Roman Catholicism, where orthodoxy was challenged by the historical inquiries and conclusions of the "modernists." In this case, however, it was not only the Bible that was challenged, but the dogmas of the church. Indeed, if dogmas have developed, as historians were pointing out, how can the church still assert that its teachings are true? Furthermore, the Catholic Church was more threatened by political liberalism than was Protestantism. The growth of the secular state, public nonreligious education, and other institutions that embodied liberal ideals was a serious challenge to the traditional authority of the church. Politically, this culminated in the events of 1870, when the pope lost Rome and the papal states to the kingdom of Italy.[38]

In response to all this, the Catholic Church retrenched to Type A theology in its strictest forms and developed an increasingly rigid system of authority. The doctrine of papal infallibility was promulgated by the First Vatican Council in the same year the pope lost Rome. That council, plus a series of decrees of Pius IX, who was then pope, affirmed a final and immutable authority—that of the pope—which was above the doubts engendered by historical research or the vicissitudes of political upheavals. The Catholic "modernists" were silenced, and with that action the church thought it had responded to the challenge of liberalism.

As we move into the twentieth century, the various continuations of Protestant fundamentalism and traditional Catholicism clearly belong to Type A theology, while a number of distinguished theologians have issued new versions of Type B.

Among the latter, Paul Tillich and Rudolf Bultmann deserve special attention. Although their theological systems vary greatly, both fall squarely within Type B and therefore may be used to exemplify the variety of forms and contents this type of theology may take.

To show that Tillich belongs to the tradition of Type B,[39] it should suffice to look at the table of contents of his *History of Christian Thought*,[40] where more space is devoted to Pseudo-Dionysius than to Thomas Aquinas; to Neoplatonism than to Tertullian; and Irenaeus gets no more than passing references as an anti-Gnostic writer. Tillich's famous "method of correlation" harkens back to Origen, whose own method was very similar—although Tillich adds existentialist dimensions quite foreign to the great Alexandrian. The following words, typical of Tillich's understanding of God, remind us of the Ineffable One of the Neoplatonists, or the Being "beyond all essence" of Erigena:

> The ground of being cannot be found within the totality of beings, nor can the ground of essence and existence participate in the tensions and disruptions characteristic of the transition from essence to existence. . . . God does not exist. He is being-itself beyond essence and existence. Therefore, to argue that God exists is to deny him.[41]

Likewise, Tillich's tendency to equate sin and the human predicament with finitude and existence, and to speak of the Fall as "the transition from essence to existence,"[42] are characteristic of Type B theology. The same could be said of his understanding of the work of Christ, his eschatology—or lack of it—and so on.

While the theology of Bultmann was quite different from that of Tillich,[43] it too should be understood as a modern expression of Type B, although now under the aegis of Heidegger's existentialism rather than of Neoplatonism. In rejecting an understanding of the work of Christ as "a mixture of sacrificial and juridical analogies, which have ceased to be tenable for us to-day,"[44] Bultmann clearly is reacting against the traditional orthodoxy of Type A. But his suggestion of a demythologized reading of the New Testament is as much a reflection of Heidegger's existentialism as Origen's reading was a reflection of the Platonism of his time.

Thus, Type B theology in various forms has continued to be present in the twentieth century, particularly in academic circles, usually as an attempt to present Christianity in terms that are more compatible with the modern mentality.

At the same time, in some circles there has been a growing emphasis on the traditional orthodoxies of Type A. The "religious right," with its combination of fundamentalism and political conservatism, is a contemporary form of Type A theology. It too sees Christianity in terms of rules of morality—a morality more individual than social or corporate. To be "born again" is to have Christ pay for one's sins and try to sin no more. "Holiness" becomes a fundamental concern of a number of these groups—"holiness" understood as personal morality, leaving out much of the biblical sense of the sacred, the covenant community, the holiness of creation, and such.

Many explanations have been given for this resurgence. Without denying the validity of such interpretations, it might be well to consider a parallel between the latter half of the twentieth century in the United States and the time when Type A theology became entrenched in the West—the time of Gregory the Great.

As we have seen, Type A became particularly attractive when many of the traditional certainties of Roman society collapsed, and the church took upon itself the task of offering new certainties and maintaining law and order.

This new form of Type A theology has become prevalent in the United States at a time when many traditional certainties are fading. The United States, once the richest nation on earth, has joined the ranks of debtor nations. The land of promise and abundance, where pockets of poverty were considered an anomaly that eventually would be wiped out, now sees those pockets increasing. After the momentous changes and hopes of the 1950s and 1960s, racial tension is once again on the rise. Vast sections of our cities have become jungles of fear, where traditional certainties and values have collapsed, just as they did at the time of the invasion of barbarians. Certain segments of the population, no longer trusting society's ability to protect them and fearing those they view as barbarians, are arming themselves against this perceived threat—just as they did after the collapse of *pax romana*. Under such circumstances, it is not surprising that a significant segment of the population finds Type A theology, with its certainties and emphasis on law and order, particularly attractive.

Thus the twentieth century has seen the continuation and revival of both Type A and Type B theologies. As has often been the case throughout the history of Christian thought, those who propose Type B accuse the others of being ignorant and narrow-minded, while the others doubt the depth of their opponents' faith and commitment to the gospel.

When viewed from a historical perspective, this debate is not the most significant feature of twentieth-century theology. Indeed, it is little more than a repetition and reenactment of similar controversies in the past.

The most significant feature of twentieth-century theology— the enormous impact of which will be seen only in the twenty-first century—is the current rediscovery, along very different routes, of the perspectives and insights characteristic of Type C theology.

PART THREE

Contemporary Relevance

*T*HROUGH a number of circumstances, the twentieth century has come to a significant recovery of Type C theology. This may be seen in such disparate phenomena as the renewal of Reformed theology through the influence of Barth, the new currents in Lutheranism represented by Lundensian theology, the liturgical renewal, the Second Vatican Council, and liberation theology. While vast differences exist among these, they have in common a return to Type C theology. Thus, it is possible to look at the wide multiplicity of theological outlooks of the twentieth century, and see a rediscovery of Type C theology.

IX

Type C Theology in the
Twentieth Century

Although the current controversies and clashes between various forms of fundamentalism and liberalism, particularly in the United States, occupy the foreground of public attention, from the long-range historical perspective, our age is marked by three further developments of far greater import for the life of the church.

The first of these is the existence, for the first time in history, of a Christian church that is universal—not only in its theological self-understanding, but in actual fact. At the beginning of the twentieth century, the numeric strength of Christianity was concentrated in Europe and the western hemisphere. At that time, roughly half of all Christians were Europeans, and four-fifths were white. At present, only one-fourth of all Christians are European, and the majority are not white.[1] Furthermore, just a few decades ago, most Christians in Africa and Asia lived under conditions of political and ecclesiastical colonialism. In Latin America, the Roman Catholic Church was notoriously weak and unproductive, while Protestantism was limited to small churches which received most of their support and directives from the United States or Europe.

This situation has changed radically in the last six or seven decades. Pope Pius XI consecrated the first Chinese bishops in 1926. By the time of the Second Vatican Council (1963–1965), only 46 percent of the prelates were from Europe, Canada, and the United States. A few decades ago, the vast majority of Protestant churches in what were called "mission lands" were organically part of churches in the United States or the United Kingdom. Today those churches are fully autonomous. In Latin

America, for instance, a number of self-governing Methodist and Presbyterian churches were formerly part of their mother denominations in the United States. Furthermore, Christianity's greatest numeric growth is taking place in the former "mission" territories.

What has happened is that the "missionary movement" has succeeded. During the nineteenth century, Protestant missionaries from Europe and the United States set out to found churches in every nation of the globe. By the end of the century, that task was largely accomplished. As mission historian Stephen Neill points out, "Though many Christians at the beginning of this century probably did not realize it, the Church had undergone in the nineteenth century one of the greatest revolutions in all its long history. It was no longer a Western religion; it had grown to be a world-wide fellowship."[2]

What had been well begun in the nineteenth century was completed in the first half of the twentieth. At the turn of the century, most of the younger churches were carbon copies of their founding bodies; while native leadership was being developed, most key positions still were held by expatriates. In a number of cases, these younger churches were seen as foreign enclaves in the countries where they existed.

All this has changed drastically. The "younger" churches often exhibit a dynamism that rivals or exceeds that of their parent bodies. As these words are being written, I have received two publications. One, from The United Methodist Church in the United States, informs us that this denomination continues its numeric decline. The other, from a Methodist church overseas, rues the fact that it is growing only at an annual rate of 5 percent! At the same time, a number of autochthonous Protestant churches have arisen all over the globe, and these often outnumber and outgrow the more traditional bodies.

It is ironic that today there are movements in the United States which wish to return to those times of missionary glory. But to send the same kind of missionaries we did fifty years ago, to do the same task, implies that the task was not done, when all facts indicate the opposite. The missionary movement *did* succeed. It is precisely because it succeeded, and strong churches now exist in practically every country to which missionaries went, that new forms of mission must be found.

If we fail to see this and insist on continuing a task that is already for the most part accomplished, three things are clear: First, it is evident that we do not believe the earlier missionaries really did what they set out to do; second, we do not trust our sisters and brothers in the younger churches with mission in their own lands; third, we are not necessarily motivated by the biblical imperative of mission, but by feelings of national and cultural superiority which make it necessary that we should always be at the giving end of faith, with others at the receiving end.

In short, the first great fact we must take into account as we look at theology and the life of the church in the last days of the twentieth century, is that a truly worldwide church exists—one in which the North Atlantic is progressively reduced from a position of absolute leadership to one of partnership in the global mission.

The second great fact of our times is what many have called the end of the Constantinian era. Since the conversion of Constantine back in the fourth century, the church has generally existed under favorable conditions, supported by society and the state. Obviously, this is an oversimplification. During the Middle Ages, vast number of Christians lived beyond the borders of Christendom under Persian or Moslem rule. At the time of the Reformation, Catholics, Lutherans, and Reformed churches enjoyed the protection of some states, but were persecuted in others. Anabaptists were persecuted by most. In every generation, Christians in one place or another have faced prejudice. Still, in general terms, it is true that throughout most of its history, Christianity has enjoyed the support of powerful empires and civilizations.

It is also true that support has been eroding since the sixteenth century; this erosion has reached new heights in the twentieth. In the sixteenth century, the Reformation brought about a situation in which Christians of different persuasions sought the exclusive support of various states—a situation which culminated in the Thirty Years' War. By the late eighteenth century, the French and American revolutions had shaken the traditional association of church and state. In the nineteenth, the pope lost his status as a civil ruler—eventually restored in the tiny Vatican City. Early in the twentieth century, the Russian and Mexican revolutions completely severed ties between church and state; later, revolutions in other nations would follow suit.

In the United States, this process has been less noticeable, but true nevertheless. Separation of church and state did not prevent various kinds of support for significant sectors of the church—tax exemptions for religious institutions, prohibition of alcoholic beverages, blue laws, prayer in school, and so on. In general, while the state was not officially Christian, society seemed to promote values that were essentially Christian. This is now being questioned both by the right—in the struggle to restore prayer in schools, for instance; and by the left—in the opposition to the arms race and intervention in Nicaragua. What must be clear to both sides, in any case, is that the argument that a particular policy is required by "Christian values" no longer produces much result in the political arena. The post-Constantinian era is progressively coming to the United States.

As was to be expected, Christians have not been of one mind in their reaction to these developments. In the nineteenth century, while most Protestants welcomed the political changes, the Roman Catholic Church, under the leadership of Pius IX, took the opposite tack. His *Syllabus of Errors* listed as errors practically all the advances of liberal democracy—such as religious freedom, separation of church and state, public education. In more recent times, divergent attitudes have appeared among Protestants—some rejoice in the new order, others mourn the old, and most do not know whether to rejoice or to mourn.

Many Third World churches are better equipped to deal with the new circumstances, for they were not part of the now crumbling Constantinian arrangement. Although it is true that the missionary movement of the nineteenth century was closely associated with colonialism, that association was not unambiguous. Interest in India was awakened by Britain's growing colonial interests in that subcontinent. William Carey (1761–1834) is usually credited as the founder of modern missions. Presumably, many an Indian prospect reacted to Carey and his fellow missionaries as if they had the power of the British East Indian Company behind them. Yet, that company saw Carey and his friends as irritants that could jeopardize its commercial interests. It was for that reason that Carey eventually settled in Serampore, which was not under the company's jurisdiction.

Similar ambiguous situations existed throughout the world. In any case, whatever moral or material support the nascent churches received from the colonial system was counterbalanced by indigenous social and cultural traditions that often ostracized new converts. Particularly as nationalism grew and the various colonial empires collapsed, converts in many younger churches knew they were not joining an organization with social and political support. They also realized that the support of the colonial system was a millstone around their neck, and they worked to create truly national churches, independent of such support. Therefore the post-Constantinian era has come as no surprise to them.

Whether in the traditionally Christian North Atlantic or in the younger churches of Africa, Asia, and Latin America, these circumstances have led many Christians to greater sympathy and understanding of the early centuries of the church, when it did not have—nor did it expect—the support of the state, or even of public opinion. As we shall see, this in turn has made such Christians much more open to the insights of that earlier period, and of Type C theology, which developed under circumstances similar to ours, and which began to decline precisely as the Constantinian arrangement progressed.

A third major development of our times, one closely related to the two we have just discussed, is the declining prestige of the North. During the last century, when people spoke of "the white man's burden" to share Christianity, as well as all the advantages of Western civilization, with the rest of the world, many among the so-called heathen reluctantly agreed with such an assessment. The industrial and military technology of the North Atlantic had proved vastly superior to that of the rest of the world and had repeatedly humiliated such proud nations as China and Japan. In South America, even Bolivar was such an admirer of the British that for a time he thought of placing the former Spanish colonies under British tutelage, which supposedly would make them ready for progress and democracy. Wherever steamships and railroads arrived, they brought marvels of Western civilization, a new understanding of the world, the collapse of ancient kingdoms and aristocracies, and dreams of progress without bounds.

Such reactions were not limited to the "backward tribes," but were shared by the vast majority in the North Atlantic. There was a very clear expectation that progress would lead humanity to unprecedented heights, a golden age of abundance, health, and peace. Possibilities without number or limit appeared positive and promising.

Then began the great disillusionment. The colonial expansionism of a number of European powers, having little left to conquer overseas, turned its attention to the Balkans, where the declining Ottoman Empire was being dismembered. Their rivalries led to a war such as the world had never seen—a war of such magnitude and devastation that at first historians called it the Great War. For the first time in human history, practically the whole world was involved. Casualties, both military and civilian, mounted to incredible numbers—mostly on the basis of that same North Atlantic technological prowess. In Europe, many began to feel that the unbounded hopes of the previous years were, to say the least, premature and probably completely unfounded. In other parts of the world, nationalist anticolonial movements gained new impetus as it became apparent that the colonies were made to suffer for issues that were entirely foreign to them.

That war, however, soon had to be renamed. After a short period of relative peace, an even greater war broke out. The Great War was now called World War I, and the new conflagration, World War II. The name itself was ominous. Were these only the beginning of a series of wars, with ever increasing levels of devastation? When would World War III begin? This question became most awesome when the destructive potential of technology was revealed in the last days of World War II. Hiroshima, Nagasaki—entire cities were practically wiped out by a single explosion.

World War II was followed by the Cold War. Except in western Europe and Japan, little effort was expended to rebuild what had been destroyed. Instead, the two great powers which emerged out of that war, the Soviet Union and the United States, became involved in an unprecedented arms race. After a few years, the bombs that had destroyed cities seemed like toys in comparison with new artifacts of destruction. Soon each of the two major contenders possessed enough firepower to destroy all human life on earth, several times over. Still the race did not stop. Since the early days of the Cold War, those two nations, with their major allies, have followed a policy of peace by terror—or as it usually is called, nuclear deterrence.

In the rest of the world, the fact that the various powers of the North have been involved in an apparently endless war has not done much to increase the prestige of those powers or of the civilization they represent. To make matters worse, the policy of nuclear deterrence, which has brought relative peace to the North Atlantic, has meant that its rivalries are now fought out by proxy in dozens of wars in other parts of the world.*

As United Methodist bishops have pointed out,[3] nuclear arsenals have not helped to prevent coventional wars. Pierre Trudeau has counted 130 wars in the Third World since 1945, with a net result of 35 million dead.[4] Such wars are not unrelated to the policies of nuclear deterrence, for a vast number are, in truth, proxy wars in which the superpowers confront each other through their clients. It is estimated that in 1987, the total military expenditure of the world was 900 billion dollars. The vast majority of such expenditures was incurred by the superpowers, their allies, and their client states. At the same time, entire regions are suffering from extreme poverty, which leads to hunger, malnutrition, ill health, and mental retardation.

In the last decades, humankind has begun to confront the cost

---

*It may seem strange that I prefer to speak in terms of North and South rather than East and West. Clearly, very significant differences exist between East and West. On the other hand, for the vast majority of the global population, the differences between the "developed" North and the "underdeveloped" South loom more urgently. From that perspective, what we call the East-West conflict appears to be more between the Northeast and Northwest, in which the South is the inevitable loser.

of modern "progress." Without denying the value of such developments as new medical technologies and greater ease in communication, it is becoming increasingly apparent that much of this progress has left behind substantial portions of the human race. In many cases it has been achieved at the expense of entire ecological systems. It also has become apparent that the globe cannot sustain the style of life of the so-called developed countries. If the entire world were to be "developed" as the North Atlantic now is, with a car for every two or three citizens and expressways crisscrossing the countryside, how long would we be able to breath? If the entire world produced industrial and other waste at the same rate as the "developed" world, how long would the oceans live? These questions, which to some in the "developed" world may seem strange, are constantly asked by Christians in the Third World, as they struggle with the shape of the future they should be trying to build.

Given such circumstances, it is not surprising that many have given up on the promises of the North—both Northeast and Northwest. Nor would it be fair to say that those who have given up are all communists or radicals of one kind or another. Many are sincere, committed, loving Christians who, a few years ago, thought the best thing they could do for their own societies was to follow the example of the North Atlantic. They have become disillusioned with that example and are looking for alternatives for living out their faith in their own situation.

Those three factors—the growth of a truly universal church; the post-Constantinian character of our times; the failure of the promises of the North—confront Christians everywhere, not just in the Third World. An increasing number find themselves in situations similar to those that prevailed before the time of Constantine. The status of a faithful Christian, or even of a church leader, no longer commands great respect as in ages past. The church no longer can count on public schools or the mores of society to teach Christian values and nurture its young in a Christian understanding of life. Increasing numbers of Christians find themselves at odds with the prevalent views and practices in the market and the workplace. Many simply capitulate or decide that their faith is a private matter, quite apart from their daily lives. But many continue to struggle and thus come to a deeper understanding of the faith—one that more closely resembles Type C theology.

This has happened both in the traditionally Christian North Atlantic and in the "younger churches" of the Third World. The new Type C theology, like its earlier counterpart, does not see Christianity primarily as a way to get to heaven. Rather, it is a clue that gives us a glimpse into God's purposes for human history and invites us to participate in those purposes. Oppressed blacks in South Africa, impoverished peasants in Central and South America, women in Europe and the United States who have discovered new realities, Christians in Europe who deal with the challenges and destruction of two wars—all have come to parallel theological outlooks.

The first sign of this new kind of theology is found in the writings of Karl Barth.[5] Barth had been trained in the best liberal theology of his time and, at the time of the First World War, discovered that what he had learned had little to do with the bitter realities of life. The theology he began to explore in his *Commentary on Romans,* and which came to full fruition in *Church Dogmatics,* rejected the facile liberalism of previous generations. But in general, Barth did not return to the rigid systems of Protestant orthodoxy. On the contrary, he developed a different sort of theology, one which progressively relied on the Word of God—none other than the very God—as its only source and authority. This theology again placed history and eschatology on center stage and thus opened the way for a fuller rediscovery of Type C.

True, the early Barth's response to the challenge of liberalism was reminiscent of Type A. In his effort to destroy the liberal notion that human progress was somehow leading us toward the divine, he insisted on the discontinuity between the divine and the human. This insistence was often couched in terms of faithfulness to the orthodox Calvinistic tradition, with its emphasis on total depravity and the distance between the divine and the human. That distance is such, he maintained in his early years, that God's grace does not even find a "point of contact" in fallen human nature. In the midst of that controversy, rejecting what he called "the theology of the *and*"—revelation and reason, revelation and religious consciousness, and so on—his words are very similar to those of Tertullian's rejection of any relationship between Athens and Jerusalem, or between the Academy and the church.[6]

As time went by, Barth came to mollify this position, especially as what has been called his "Christological concentration" led him to the conclusion that it is necessary to think of both God and humans in different terms. By 1956, he delivered lectures on "The Humanity of God," in which he nuanced much of what he had said in his earlier polemic against liberalism and the various forms of "theologies of the and." He explained that he opposed a theology that thought God could somehow be known through a study of human piety. Then he asked himself if, in speaking of God as the "wholly other," he had not left aside other important emphases:

> But did it not appear to escape us by quite a distance that the *deity* of the *living* God—and we certainly wanted to deal with him—found its meaning and its power only in the context of His history and of His dialogue with *man,* and thus in His *togetherness* with man? Indeed—and this is the point back of which we cannot go—it is a matter of *God's* sovereign togetherness with man, a togetherness grounded in Him and determined, delimited, and ordered through Him alone. . . . . In Jesus Christ there is no isolation of man from God or of God from man. Rather, in Him we encounter the history, the dialogue, in which God and man meet together and are together, the reality of the covenant *mutually* contracted, preserved, and fulfilled by them.[7]

Barth made these statements on the basis of what God has done and revealed in Jesus Christ, which increasingly became the center of his theology: "We do not need to engage in a free-ranging investigation to seek out and construct who and what God truly is, but only to read the truth about both where it resides—namely, in the fullness of their togetherness, their covenant which proclaims itself in Jesus Christ."[8]

It is clear that here we move closer to much of what we found in the theology of Irenaeus: History as the context—the sole context—of God's revelation; that what it means to be truly human is known only in the incarnate Word, Jesus Christ, for it is precisely in that relationship with God that humanity finds its true being.

By the time Barth wrote the words above, others among the younger theologians were carrying Christological doctrine to similar conclusions. Most notable was Dietrich Bonhoeffer,[9] who was killed by the Nazis a few days before the end of the World War II. In his writings one finds much that reminds us of Type C theology: that "the Church is Christ existing as community"; the call for a world-affirming Christianity, on the basis of the incarnation; and perhaps the enigmatic references in his *Letters and Papers from Prison* to a "world come of age."

It was from Bonhoeffer that more recent theology took its cue: that the "secularization of God" in Christ must lead us toward an understanding in which we see God's action in the events of secular history. By 1961, Wolfhart Pannenberg had made a very strong case for abolishing the traditional distinction between "world history" and "history of salvation."[10] This interest in history also played an important part in the Marxist-Christian dialogue and in the work of the theologians most involved in it, Joseph Hromàdka and Jan Lochman.[11] The contemporary German theologian most noted for his recovery of the centrality of Christian eschatology, Jürgen Moltmann,[12] declared that much of his rediscovery of the Christian notion of hope came through his personal dialogue with the famous book on hope by Marxist philosopher Ernst Bloch.[13] In any case, it is significant that history once again has been placed at the very center of Reformed theology—as it was much earlier in the theology we have called Type C.

While these developments were taking place among German Reformed theologians, Lutheran tradition in Sweden was also moving in directions that would lead it to a rediscovery of Type C. This is called Lundensian theology, since it occurred around the University of Lund. The Lundensians were not convinced by the typical nineteenth-century interpretation which thought of Luther as the founder of modernity and of German bourgeois liberalism as his most faithful exponent.

The studies of the early leading figures of the Lundensian school, Anders Nygren and Gustav Aulén, both versed in historical theology, resulted in a very different picture. The Luther they discovered was neither the liberal father of the German nation nor the rigid figure of Protestant orthodoxy. They found that the powers of evil played a very important role in Luther's theology—something that was true of neither liberalism nor traditional orthodoxy. They realized that for Luther, redemption was not a principle or a doctrine, but a drama—a struggle which takes place in the death and resurrection of Jesus.

The Lundensians also set out to discover the roots of Luther's theology in earlier thought—especially in patristic thought. They did not look at particular doctrines, but rather at fundamental motifs found both in Luther and in the earliest Christian writers. Along these lines, Aulén's *Christus Victor* was of fundamental importance, for it was Aulén who first made clear that the dominant view in the early church regarding the work of Christ is that he has overcome the powers of evil. Aulén's argument that the same was true for Luther may be somewhat overstated. The important point is that here was one of the central doctrines of Christianity on which the early church—and Irenaeus in particular—held a position different from the main alternatives offered by later theology.

Thus Lundensian theology brought to the foreground several important insights of Type C: The human predicament is our enslavement to the power of sin; the work of Christ consists in conquering that power and liberating us from it; this work centers on the cross, and also on the incarnation and the resurrection—all this understood in a historical and corporate sense, not in the individualistic and psychologizing sense of Bultmann and much of the existentialist tradition.

While these developments were taking place in Protestant theology, some Catholic theologians were moving in parallel directions.[14] During most of the twentieth century, the official stance of the Catholic Church was a continuation of the rigid rejection of modernity that had taken place in the nineteenth. Theologians needed to be careful not to step out of bounds.

Indeed, several of the most creative theologians of the period—some of whom later became advisors to the Second Vatican Council—were prohibited from publishing their views for varying periods of time.

In such circumstances, a significant contribution was made by Henri de Lubac and Jean Daniélou in the series *Sources Chrétiennes*. The more conservative elements in the church accused them of choosing for publication those early Christian writers who most brought into question established scholastic theology—Irenaeus among them.

In the long run, a new generation of theologians nurtured in this early Christian theology would arise in France as well as elsewhere. Pierre Teilhard de Chardin, silenced by the Vatican, offered a Christian understanding of evolution very different from Darwin's. His vision of Christ as the *homo futurus*, the goal of all evolution, brings to mind some of the passages in which Irenaeus speaks of Adam and Eve as being created after the model of the incarnate Word. In a similar vein, Karl Rahner, the most influential Catholic theologian of the century, spoke of the incarnation as the goal of all creation, not simply as God's response to sin—another theme to be found in Irenaeus.

Thus, it is not surprising that when the Second Vatican Council met and these various undercurrents were allowed to surface, much of what the Council said and did was quite consonant with Type C theology. Indeed, history stands at the very center of the Christian message as the Council understood it, and Christ's "recapitulation" stands at the center of history: "The Word of God, through whom all things were made, became man and dwelt among men: a perfect man, he entered world history, taking that history into himself and recapitulating it."[15]

While it would be wrong to claim that the Council declared itself in favor of a particular type of theology, it is clear that in case after case, the perspectives of Type C have made an impact. As one reads the Council's documents, the impression one receives is that the Christian message, rather than a set of laws or doctrines, is a view of history—a history brought into being by a loving God, put into human hands for development, and brought to its final fulfillment in Jesus Christ and his final revelation. The church is seen as involved in a common history with the rest of humankind. In this pilgrimage, the church is nourished by the sacrament of communion, which relates not only to the cross, but also to God's future.

While Vatican II did not opt for a particular type of theology, its use of Type C perspectives gave further strength to the rediscovery of that type. Catholic theologians who had already moved in such directions felt they were given permission to continue along that route. This was most evident in the assembly of Latin American Catholic bishops in Medellín, Colombia, in 1968, which gave impetus to Latin American liberation theology.

Liberation theologies—not only Latin American, but black, feminist, and others—have moved naturally in the direction of Type C. Since all have developed from the perspective of those who are excluded and expect a new order, the category of history is fundamental to all such theologies[16]—not history as an academic discipline, but history as the concrete scene of human life and endeavor. As in earlier Type C theology, liberation theologies tend to emphasize concrete truth—historical truth—above abstract generalities. Indeed, many liberation theologians express the suspicion that so-called universal truths often are nothing but truth as seen from the perspective of the powerful. Christianity does not consist in a series of doctrines or rules, but in the action of God incarnate in history.

Based on this centrality of history and on the theologians' involvement in it, liberation theologies have rediscovered Type C at several other points—for instance, their keen awareness of the powers of evil. When liberation theologians speak of racism, sexism, or neocolonialism, they are not speaking, as others often think, merely of the sum total of the attitudes of racists, sexists, or neocolonialists. They are speaking of Evil—with a capital E—Evil, whose work is not mysterious, but whose power often is.

Within this context, it is not surprising that many liberation theologians speak of Christ as the victor, the conqueror, or the liberator. Nor is it surprising that the new liturgies coming out of

Latin America focus not so much on the death of Christ as on his incarnation, resurrection, and final reign.

Finally, it is significant that the characteristic hermeneutic tool of liberation theologies is typology. Scripture speaks to us because somehow we find in it types or figures of our own history: God, calling the people out of Egypt; Second Isaiah, promising a return from captivity; Mary, singing that the mighty shall be put down; Jesus, placing a child at the center; God, using the poor and foolish in the early church to shame the rich and wise—these are typical of God's actions now.

All these various currents of the rediscovery of Type C would have had less impact on the everyday life of the church, had not another movement affected our Sunday services: liturgical renewal. Historians of liturgy, as well as historians of theology, have long been aware that there is a connection between the way the church worships and what the church believes. Worship both expresses and shapes theology. In recent times, the rediscovery of worship as it was practiced in the ancient church has given the new forms of Type C theology a vehicle for expression and a nurturing atmosphere.

During much of the twentieth century there has been a continual search for liturgical practices that more nearly express the faith of the church. This quest has taken many different directions: the Roman Catholic return to the mass in the vernacular; new hymnody among both Catholics and Protestants; a closer relationship between preaching and liturgy; the growing use of the liturgical year and the lectionary among Protestants.

Probably the most significant single element, however, has been the recovery of ancient Christian liturgical practices. Through historical research, we now know much more about the practice of baptism and communion in the first centuries of the Christian church than was known two or three generations ago. A significant step in this direction was the final attribution to Hippolytus of an ancient document. Hippolytus, who lived in Rome, was himself part of the transition from Type C to Type A.[17] As most Type A theologians, he considered himself a defender of traditional views, and scholars believe that the liturgy he describes in that document may well reflect the practices of an earlier time. Had he known of any recent innovations, he certainly would have challenged them. This places the practices he describes roughly at the time of Irenaeus and Tertullian. It is also significant that Tertullian, on the other side of the Mediterranean and a few years earlier, offered a description of baptism in most points similar to that of Hippolytus.

Based on these witnesses, and on many other pieces of fragmentary evidence, scholars have reconstructed much of the liturgy of the church in the second and third centuries—the time just before the conversion of Constantine. This research has progressively influenced individuals and committees charged with developing liturgical resources for various denominations, and as a result, a widespread consensus has begun to emerge which not only reflects the practices of the church at a much earlier time, but also proves quite supportive of Type C theology.

Two examples should suffice. Baptism is gaining new significance as Christians come to a greater realization of the growing chasm between their faith and the faith of society at large. Not only in the younger churches, but also in many of the more established ones, the proportion of adults who request baptism, as compared with infants who receive it, is increasing. More and more, embracing of the Christian faith is becoming a conscious—and potentially costly—decision. Such was also the case in the early church. In order to dramatize this, the baptismal liturgy included an act of renunciation, in which the neophyte rejected the Devil and all his works. Obviously, the theological setting for this act was a view of history as the great battleground between God and the powers of evil; and of baptism as being grafted into the body of the victorious and resurrected Head, Jesus Christ—one reason baptism was usually celebrated at Easter.

It is significant that a similar act is included in a number of recently developed services of baptism. The document *Baptism, Eucharist and Ministry* of the World Council of Churches lists "a renunciation of evil" among the elements that should find a place in "any comprehensive order of baptism."[18] In 1976, The

United Methodist Church published a new service for baptism in which the candidate is asked, "Do you renounce the bondage of sin and the injustices of this world?"[19] Likewise, in the new order for baptism of the Presbyterian Church (U.S.A.) the candidate is asked, "Do you renounce evil, and its power in the world, which defies God's righteousness and love? . . . Do you renounce the ways of sin that separate you from the love of God?"[20] Similar acts of renunciation may be found also in Catholic, Lutheran, and Anglican liturgies.

The eucharistic service also has undergone similar changes. Most "traditional" Western liturgies derived from medieval practices when communion was seen as relating almost exclusively to the passion of Christ and therefore took on funereal overtones. In contrast, communion in the early church was indeed a celebration, relating not only nor primarily to the passion, but above all, to the resurrection of Jesus and his return in final glory. The new liturgies have returned to that earlier understanding and practice. There is a marked contrast between the opening of the communion service as it appears, with slight variations, in most traditional liturgies—"All ye who do truly and earnestly repent of your sins"—and the opening sentence in the Presbyterian *Worshipbook,* typical of the newer services: "Friends: This is the joyful feast of the people of God!"

Both these services—baptism and communion—now suggest a view which combines the joy of Christian faith with a sober realization that the present order is not the Kingdom, that Christians are still called to do battle in a world which—contrary to what the Constantinian arrangement would have us believe—is still hostile to the gospel. We rejoice because Christ has risen; we must suffer with him because he has not yet returned. This is the central perspective of Type C theology, one that is becoming increasingly needed in the new circumstances in which the church finds itself at the close of the twentieth century.

There is no doubt that this rediscovery of Type C produces dissonance and disruption. Like the man who voiced the complaint, "They have taken away the sanctity of communion and turned it into a party," many people are being led to liturgical practices that do not fit their theological perspectives. Those who see the Christian faith as a matter of law, sin, debt, and payment will draw little comfort from "the joyful feast of the people of God" unless some of their theological presuppositions are changed.

At the same time, millions of Christians in situations in which they must constantly struggle against a hostile world, seeking to change its structures and practices so as to bring it to closer conformity with God's will, find strong reassurance in such a service. The pastor who could not be classified because she was neither liberal nor conservative was interpreting Scripture from the perspective of a modern form of Type C theology. Likewise, the professor who believed that Isaiah 53 referred to Israel at the time of the writing, but that it also applies to Jesus, was simply interpreting Scripture in the typological fashion characteristic of Type C.

And what of the doctor who declared he could no longer hold the faith of his fundamentalist upbringing or that of his liberal professor? He was perplexed because his faith apparently had little to do with a setting in which he dealt constantly with the marvels of technology and the possibilities of its misuse. Perhaps he could be helped by a theological outlook that would allow him to see God's action in history and technological advance, without losing sight of the demonic dimension also present in all human history—including technology.

As the twentieth century draws to a close, it is my expectation that the twenty-first will see a fuller rediscovery of what I have called Type C, as humankind continues to struggle with the crucial issues of justice and peace. Perhaps I am mistaken, and that will not be the case. But of one thing we can be certain: The Lord of history—the Lord who joined history for our sake—will still be with us, suffering with us through the calamities we bring upon ourselves and our children, calling us—always calling us—to join him in the miracle and the hope of his resurrection. So be it!

Notes

Notes to Introduction

1. Justo L. Gonzalez, *History of Christian Thought* (Nashville: Abingdon, 1970-1975), 3 vols.; rev. ed., 1987. Future references will make use of the revised edition, abbreviated as *History*.

Notes to Chapter I

1. W.H.C. Frend, *The Donatist Church: A Movement of Protest in Roman North Africa* (Oxford: Clarendon, 1952) has explored and demonstrated how this social structure was reflected in religious issues in and around Carthage. See esp. pp. 333-36.
2. See *History*, 1:171, n. 1.
3. The *Martyrdom of Perpetua and Felicitas*, at least in its present form, is probably the work of Tertullian. There is some room for doubt, however, and also the possibility that Tertullian—or another—edited an earlier document.
4. I say "probably," because there is some debate among scholars as to the possibility that the *Octavius* of Minucius Felix may have been earlier. I have summarized the bibliography on this matter in *History*, 1:184, n. 44. In any case, even granting the possibility that the *Octavius* may be earlier than Tertullian's *Apology*, the theological importance of the former is minimal, and therefore Tertullian remains the first significant Christian author in Latin.
5. On the rhetorical structure of Tertullian's arguments, see R. D. Sider, *Ancient Rhetoric and the Art of Tertullian* (Oxford University Press, 1971); see also R. D. Sider, "Tertullian, *On the Shows:* An Analysis," JTS 1978, pp. 339-65.
6. *De test. anim.* 6 (ANF, 3:179).
7. See *History*, 1:174, n. 8; see also D. Michaelides, *Foi, Ecriture et tradition: Les Praescriptiones chez Tertullian* (Paris: Editions Aubier-Montagne, 1969).
8. *Apol.* 2 (ANF, 3:18).
9. *Praesc.* 7 (ANF, 3:246).
10. *History*, 1:174, n. 6.
11. See *History*, 1:63-65.
12. Latin text in Daniel Ruiz Bueno, ed., *Actas de los Mártires* (Madrid: Biblioteca de Autores Cristianos, 1968), p. 252.
13. *Hist. eccl.* 2.16.
14. On the other hand, some scholars tend to deny the eclectic nature of middle Platonism. See J. Dillon, *The Middle Platonists* (London: Duckworth, 1977).
15. See F. Coplestone, *A History of Philosophy*, Vol. I: *Greece and Rome* (Westminster, Md.: Newman, 1959), pp. 451-75.
16. The best introduction to this entire tradition, especially to the manner in which it affected Christian theology in Alexandria, is still C. Bigg, *The Christian Platonists of Alexandria* (Oxford: Clarendon, 1886).

159

17. "As many men drawing down the ship, cannot be called many causes, but one cause consisting of many . . . so also philosophy, being the search for truth, contributes to the comprehension of truth. . . . So while the truth is one, many things contribute to its investigation. But its discovery is by the Son." *Strom.* 1.20 (ANF, 2:323).

18. *Strom.* 1.5.

19. A brief discussion of the environment and its impact on the New Testament may be found in John E. Stambach and David L. Balch, *The New Testament in Its Social Environment* (Philadelphia: Westminster, 1986), pp. 145-54.

20. See Glanville Downey, *A History of Antioch in Syria from Seleucus to the Arab Conquest* (Princeton: Princeton University Press, 1961); John P. Meier, "Antioch," in Raymond E. Brown and John P. Meier, *Antioch and Rome: New Testament Cradles of Catholic Christianity* (New York: Paulist, 1983), pp. 11-86; D. S. Wallace-Hadrill, *Christian Antioch: A Study of Early Christian Thought in the East* (Cambridge: Cambridge University Press, 1982); Wayne A. Meeks and Robert L. Wilken, *Jews and Christians in Antioch in the First Four Centuries of the Common Era* (Missoula, Mont.: Scholars Press, 1978).

21. Josephus, *Ant.* 12.119; *Adv. Ap.* 2.39.

22. Ignatius of Antioch, *Ad Magn.* 10:1,3; *Ad Rom.* 3:3; *Ad Phil.* 6:1.

23. *History,* 1:81, n. 82.

24. It is on the basis of Irenaeus' relationship to and dependence upon such forerunners that Loofs and others have sought to prove that a great deal of Irenaeus' work is taken from earlier writings, particularly those of Justin and Theophilus. See F. Loofs, *Theophilus von Antiochen und die anderen theologischen Quellen bei Irenaeus* (Leipzig: J. C. Hinrichs, 1930). Loof's thesis has been refuted by a number of scholars. See, e.g., A. Benoit, *Saint Irenée: Introduction à l'étude de sa théologie* (Paris: Presses Universitaires de France, 1960). In any case, the debate is only tangential to this essay, for if Irenaeus is proved to have derived a significant portion of his work from other authors, this simply confirms our thesis that his theology represents a very early understanding of the faith.

25. Their names are Greek, rather than Gaul or Roman. A.H.M. Jones, "The Economic Life of the Towns of the Roman Empire," *Recueils de la Societé Jean Bodin* (1955), pp. 182-83, has studied the merchant community of Lyon and has come to the conclusion that many came from the East, even from as far as Syria. None of those he was able to trace were native-born. Thus the question remains open: Did the Christians settle in Lyon for economic reasons, such as trade, or were they fleeing persecution—or both? Given the nature of our sources, that question is impossible to answer with any degree of certainty.

26. Quoted by Eusebius, *Hist. eccl.* 5.20 (NPNF, Second Series, 1:238-39).

27. For a description of Antiochene Christology and its course during the controversies of the fourth and fifth centuries, see *History,* 1:335-80. The classical study is R. V. Sellers, *Two Ancient Christologies: A Study in the Christological Thought of the Schools of Alexandria and Antioch in the Early History of Christian Doctrine* (London: SPCK, 1954).

28. "Irenaeus addresses all these issues {of biblical interpretation} and does so by employing the notion of a salvation that focuses on the story of the incarnate Word of God but relates that story to the Word's activity in creation

and in the history of Israel. By defining the incarnate Lord, Irenaeus clarifies the identity of the hero of the Christian story, a story that includes all of human history." Rowan A. Greer, in James L. Kugel and Rowan A. Greer, *Early Biblical Interpretation* (Philadelphia: Westminster, 1986), p. 156.

Notes to Chapter II

1. Here I am speaking of the way Christians saw pagans. For the opposite—that is, the way pagans looked at Christians, see Pierre de Labriolle, *La réaction païenne: Etude sur la polemique antichrétienne du Ier au VIe siècle* (Paris: L'Artisan du Livre, 1941); Robert L. Wilken, *The Christians as the Romans Saw Them* (New Haven: Yale University Press, 1984); Robert Lane Fox, *Pagans and Christians* (New York: Knopf, 1987).

2. The bibliography on gnosticism is endless. Regarding its origin, see *History*, 1:127, n. 16. A recent book that deserves special attention within the context of my argument is E. Pagels, *The Gnostic Gospel* (New York: Random House, 1979). Her argument that the condemnation of gnosticism and the means by which the church reacted to it served to suppress dissident voices and strengthen those in authority is quite valid. Whether this is the main reason gnosticism was condemned is open to debate. In any case, it is clear that, in reaction to gnosticism, Christianity became much more institutionalized and those in authority increased their power. It is also clear that, once the power struggle was over, a number of Gnostic traits crept back into orthodox Christianity. This is not to say that gnosticism was right or that it should not have been rejected. It is simply another instance of the manner in which theological debate and political struggle are often joined.

3. This is a stylized summary which attempts to take into account what is known of a number of different systems. For further distinctions among those systems and bibliography regarding them, see *History*, 1:126-37.

4. Views reflected and rejected in I John 4:2b-3a: "Every spirit which confesses that Jesus Christ has come in the flesh is of God, and every spirit which does not confess Jesus is not of God. This is the spirit of antichrist."

5. Views which apparently had appeared already in the Corinthian community and which Paul refutes in I Cor. 15. Note that Paul is defending not simply life after death or the immortality of the soul, but the resurrection of the body.

6. The classical study of Marcion is A. von Harnack's *Marcion: Das Evangelium vom fremden Gott: Eine Monographie zur Geschichte der Grundlegung der katholischen Kirche* (reprint, Berlin: Akademie-Verlag, 1960); also see E. C. Blackman, *Marcion and His Influence* (London: SPCK, 1948).

7. *Ep. ad Cor.* 20.11.

8. *Adv. Marc.* 1.26 (ANF, 3: 292).

9. *Ibid.* (ANF, 3:291).

10. This is the most common interpretation of Tertullian's formula and his understanding of the Trinity. See, however, G. L. Prestige, *God in Patristic Thought* (London: W. Heinemann, 1936), pp. 97-106.

11. *Adv. Marc.* 1.11. Tertullian may have lifted this argument from Irenaeus, who employs it, with less sarcasm, in *Adv. haer.* 2.30.3.

12. *Adv. Herm.* 18.

13. Tertullian does declare that there were various steps in creation: "God indeed consummated all His works in a due order. . . . For He did not at once inundate light with the splendour of the sun, nor all at once temper darkness with the moon's assuaging ray. The heaven He did not all at once bedeck with constellations and stars, nor did He at once fill the seas with their teeming monsters. The earth itself He did not endow with its varied fruitfulness all at once; but at first He bestowed upon it being, and then He filled it, that it might not be made in vain." *Adv. Herm.* 29 (ANF, 3:493).

Note, however, that all verbs here are past tense. God did create following an order, but that order was completed in the Genesis narrative.

14. This view is found consistently in Tertullian's writings. Some passages, however, are strikingly reminiscent of what we shall see in Irenaeus about God's intention that Adam and Eve should grow. Such is *Adv. Marc.* 2.4 (ANF, 3:299): "The goodness of God having, therefore, provided man for the pursuit of the knowledge of Himself . . . it first prepared a habitation for him, the vast fabric (of the world) to begin with, and then afterwards the vaster one (of a higher world) that he might on a great, as well as on a smaller scale, practise and advance in his probation, and so be promoted from the *good* which God had given him, that is, from his high position, to God's *best;* that is, to some higher abode."

15. *De anima* 40.

16. For Clement's treatment of the doctrine of God and its relation to creation, see E. F. Osborn, *The Philosophy of Clement of Alexandria* (Cambridge: University Press, 1957), pp. 25-37, which shows the degree to which Clement is consistent with his Platonic presuppositions, often at the expense of traditional religious language.

17. *De princ.* 1.1.6; *Contra Cel.* 7. 38.

18. "The doctrine of the utter unchangeableness of God set severe limits upon the understanding of other divine attributes. . . . God was required to know a changing world in an utterly unchanging way, to act upon a temporally developing world of nature and human history in a totally atemporal way, and to be so far removed from time that he contained the entire past, present and future of the universe within himself simultaneously rather than successively." Rem B. Edwards, "The Pagan Doctrine of the Absolute Unchangeableness of God," in RelSt (1978), p. 305.

19. Athanasius, *Oratio contra Ar.* 2.26. Irenaeus seems to have been aware of this difficulty in a theology based on absolute divine transcendence, as shown in his argument regarding the Gnostic Pleroma and its relationship to the universe: *Adv. haer.* 2.1.3.

20. *Dial.* 56.11.

21. See particularly Philo, *De opif.* 138; *Leg. alleg.* 1. 31. In *Adv. haer.* 1.14 and 28, Irenaeus imputes similar views to some Gnostics.

22. *De princ.* 1.3; 2.8; *Comm. in Cant., prol.; Comm. in Rom.* 2.13.

23. This leads Richard P. Hanson to declare: "The critical subject on which Origen never accepted the biblical viewpoint was the significance of history. To the writers of the Bible, history is *par excellence* the field of God's revelation of

himself. . . . To this insight Origen is virtually blind. He does not . . . reject or abandon history. . . . But he perilously reduces the significance of history, and with history, of sacraments and of eschatology. In his view, history, if it is to have any significance at all, can be no more than an acted parable." *Allegory and Event: A Study of the Sources and Significance of Origen's Interpretation of Scripture* (London: SCM, 1959), pp. 363-64.

24. *De princ.* 1.7.

25. *Strom.* 3.16.

26. *Adv. haer.* 2.13.3 (ANF, 1:374).

27. *Epid.* 8.

28. *Adv. haer.* 4, *prol.* (ANF, 1:463): "Now man is a mixed organization of soul and flesh, who was formed after the likeness of God, and moulded by His hands, that is, by the Son and the Holy Spirit."

Adv. haer. 5.1.3 (ANF, 1:527): "Never at any time did Adam escape the hands of God."

Adv. haer. 5. 6. 1 (ANF, 1:531): "For by the hands of the Father, that is, by the Son and the Holy Spirit, man, and not [merely] a part of man, was made in the likeness of God."

Epid. 11 (ACW, 16: 54): "Man He fashioned with His own hands."

29. *Adv. haer.* 2.26.1 (ANF, 1: 397).

30. *Adv. haer.* 2.25.3; 4.11.1.

31. *Adv. haer.* 2.25. 3; 4.11.1. (ANF, 1:521): "It was possible for God Himself to have made man perfect from the first, but man could not receive this [perfection], being as yet an infant. . . . God had power at the beginning to grant perfection to man; but as the latter was only recently created, he could not possibly have received it, or even if he had received it, could not have contained it, or containing it, could not have retained it."

The connection between this understanding of creation and the significance of history is made clear in the following text from *Adv. haer.* 4.39.2 (ANF, 1:522-23), which also relates all this to God's purpose of divinizing the human creature: "How, then, shall he be a god, who has not yet been made a man? Or how can he be perfect who was but lately created? . . . If, then, thou art God's workmanship, await the hand of thy Maker which creates everything in due time; in due time as far as thou art concerned, whose creation is being carried out." Cf. *Epid.* 12.

32. *Ad Autol.* 2.25.

33. *Strom.* 2.22.

34. At least until the time of Procopius of Gaza, who died in A.D. 529. See his *In Gen.* 2.8 (PG, 87:164).

35. *Epid.* 22 (ACW, 16: 61): "The 'image' is the Son of God, in whose image man was made."

Adv. haer. 5.16.2 (ANF, 1:544): "For in times long past, it was said that man was created after the image of God, but it was not yet [actually] shown; for the Word was as yet invisible, after whose image man was created." Cf. *Adv. haer.* 3.22.3; *Epid.* 97.

36. That the theme was common in early Christian theology may be shown by the following quote from Tertullian: God, "looking on Christ His Word, who was to become man, said, 'Let us make man in our own image, and after our likeness.' " *Adv. Marc.* 5.8 (ANF, 3:445).

This notion, however, is not connected organically with the rest of Tertullian's theology. It seems to be a remnant of earlier views which he accepts, but for which he has little use. His interpretation of the *imago Dei* as meaning simply that the human creature resembled God may be found in *Adv. Marc.* 2.5. Likewise, the static understanding of original human perfection may be found in *Adv. Marc.* 5.5. These are just two among many such passages that could be cited. (Irenaeus also speaks of a physical resemblance between God and humans: *Epid.* 11.)

37. *Adv. haer.* 4.14.1 (ANF, 1:478): "In the beginning, therefore, did God form Adam, not as if He stood in need of man, but that He might have [someone] upon whom to confer His benefits." This is closely related to the goal of making the human creature divine, to which we shall refer later. The child originally created was intended to receive the divine benefits; but was also intended to grow toward greater fellowship with God.

38. *Epid.* 12 (ACW, 16:55): "So, having made the man lord of the earth and of everything in it, He made him in secret lord also over the servants in it {i.e., the angels}. They, however, were in their full development, while the lord, that is, the man, was a little one; for he was a child and had need to grow so as to come to his full perfection."

There may be echoes of this in Tertullian *De pat.* 5, but the exact meaning of that text is not altogether clear. Note also that similar views of the eventual superiority of humans over angels appear in Paul (I Cor. 6:3: "Do you not know that we are to judge angels?") and in Hebrews (2:5-8).

39. Furthermore, it was jealousy of this high destiny of the human creature that led Satan to rebel. *Epid.* 16. A similar idea appears in Tertullian, when he declares that the devil "impatiently bore that the Lord God subjected the universal works which He had made to His own image, that is, to man." *De pat.* 5 (ANF, 3:709).

40. In this context, one should note that Irenaeus understands the law given in Eden as a teaching tool. *Epid.* 15. Furthermore, Christ's fulfillment of the law frees us from it. "He does not wish those who are to be redeemed to be brought under the Mosaic legislation—for the law has been fulfilled by Christ—but to go free in newness by the Word, through faith and love towards the Son of God." *Epid.* 89 (ACW, 16:102).

"We should not turn back, I mean, to the former legislation. For we have received the Lord of the Law, the Son of God; and through faith in Him we learn to love God with our whole heart, and our neighbor as ourselves. . . . Therefore we have no need of the law as pedagogue. Behold, we speak with the Father and stand face to face with Him, become infants in malice, and made strong in all justice and propriety." *Epid.* 95-96 (ACW, 16:105-6).

41. We are so used to reading the words of the Serpent in Gen. 3:5 as a lie catering to pride that this option may seem rather surprising. But it is fundamental for an understanding of Irenaeus and of his entire theological tradition. It was always intended that the human creature should grow to be "like God." The Serpent did not strictly lie, but brought humanity to a premature, and therefore monstrous, consciousness. It should be noted that in the book of Revelation, which comes from a theological background similar to that of Irenaeus, the tree of life, which was forbidden in Genesis, appears at the

center of the New Jerusalem. In the end, according to this ancient theological tradition, humans will eat of this tree which shall make them "like gods."

42. *Adv. haer.* 3.23.6 (ANF, 1:457): "Wherefore He also drove him out of Paradise, and removed him far from the tree of life, not because He envied him the tree of life, as some venture to assert, but because He pitied him [and did not desire] that he should continue a sinner for ever, nor that the sin which surrounded him should be immortal, and evil interminable and irremediable."

43. This is why Irenaeus is so insistent that Adam will be saved. *Adv. haer.* 3.23.

44. *Adv. haer.* 3.23.5.

45. *Adv. haer.* 4.22.1 This is a theme that appears repeatedly in the writings of Irenaeus, usually within the context of the victory Christ has won for us by conquering the Evil One to whom we were subject. It is not only the sin of the first parents, but also every other sin that contributes to this slavery. See, for instance, Irenaeus' discussion of the episode of the golden calf: *Adv. haer.* 4.15.1.

Notes to Chapter III

1. *De cult. fem.* 1.1; *De pud.* 13; *De jejun.* 3; *De pat.* 13. At the same time, again to avoid oversimplification, one should point out that the following words are to be found in Irenaeus: "We were debtors to none other but to Him whose commandment we had transgressed at the beginning." *Adv. haer.* 5.16.3 (ANF, 1:544).

2. *De poen.* 4 (ANF, 4:660): "It is not the fact that it is good which binds us to obey, but the fact that God has enjoined it."

3. *De poen.* 6.

4. *De pud.* 22.

5. *Adv. Prax.* 25.

6. *Ibid.* 5.

7. *Adv. Cel.* 2.2; *Adv. Marc.* 4.14-16, 34-35.

8. *De poen.* 6 (ANF, 3:662): "We are not washed in order that we may cease sinning, but because we have ceased, since in the heart we have been bathed already."

9. *Ibid.* 7.

10. *De bap.* 16 (ANF, 3:677): "These two baptisms He sent out from the wound of His pierced side, in order that they who believed in His blood might be bathed with the water; they who have been bathed in the water might likewise drink the blood. This is the baptism which both stands in lieu of the fontal bathing when it has not been received, and restores it when lost."

11. *Ibid.* 1 (ANF, 3:669): "Happy is our sacrament of water, in that, by washing away the sins of our *early* blindness, we are set free and admitted into eternal life!" (italics mine)

12. *Ibid.* 18.

13. Mand. 4.3.6.

14. *II Clem ad Cor.* 8.1-3.

15. Note, however, *Adv. Marc.* 4.40, where he uses communion to refute docetism.

16. See *De res. car.* 8.

17. *De anima* 58.

18. *Apol.* 48; *Adv. Marc.* 3.24.

19. See *History* 1:142-43.

20. *Strom.* 4.6 (ANF, 2:414): "It is the will of God [that we should attain] the knowledge of God, which is the communication of immortality."

Ibid. 4.22 (ANF 2:434): "Could we, then, suppose any one proposing to the [true—that is, orthodox] Gnostic whether he should choose the knowledge of God or everlasting salvation; and if these, which are entirely identical, were separable, he would without the least hesitation choose the knowledge of God." Cf. Origen, *Hom. in Gen.* 1.13.

21. *Strom.* 4.21 (ANF, 2:433): "Assuredly it is impossible to attain knowledge (*gnosis*) by bad conduct."

Ibid. 5.11 (ANF 2:460): "Now the sacrifice which is acceptable to God is unswerving abstraction from the body and its passions. This is really true piety."

Origen, *Peri Euches* 9.2: "The eyes of the mind arise to the point where they no longer rest on terrestrial goods, nor are they any longer full of material images. They reach such a height that they despise created things, and consider only God."

22. *De princ.* 2.9.3 (ANF, 4:288): "The understanding {or intellect}, falling away from its status and dignity, was made or named soul; and that, if repaired and corrected, it returns to the condition of the understanding."

23. *Ibid.* 1.7.5. Origen is referring here to Rom. 8:20, one of the many passages in Paul that have baffled interpreters, but that are made much clearer from the perspective of Type C theology.

24. *Ibid.* 1.2.8.

25. *Ibid.* 2.6.3.

26. This may be seen in Clement's half-hearted rejection of docetism (*Strom.* 6.9; ANF, 2:496): "In the case of the Saviour, it were ludicrous [to suppose] that the body, as a body, demanded the necessary aids in order to its duration. For He ate, not for the sake of the body, which was kept together by a holy energy, but in order that it might not enter into the minds of those who were with Him to entertain a different opinion of him; in like manner as certainly some afterwards supposed that He appeared in a phantasmal shape. But He was entirely impassible, inaccessible to any movement of feeling—either pleasure or pain."

27. *De princ.* 4.1.31.

28. *In Io.* 32.24; *Mat. ser.* 85.

29. *De princ.* 2.11.6.

30. *Ibid.* 2.10.4-6; *De orat.* 28. 13; *Hom. Num.* 16.3.

31. *De princ.* 3.6.3.

32. *Ibid.* 3.1.23. This notion of recurring worlds was one reason for his condemnation by the Fifth Ecumenical Council. It is also significant to note that Origen did not explain how those other worlds would be redeemed without new incarnations. Apparently, his orthodoxy made him shy away from the strictly logical conclusion—that an incarnation would be necessary for the illumination of each fallen world.

33. *Adv. haer.* 5.21.3 (ANF, 1:550): "For as in the beginning he {Satan}

enticed man to transgress his Maker's law, and thereby got him into his power; yet his power consists in transgression and apostasy, and with these he bound man."

34. *Ibid.* 3.22.4.

35. See the detailed discussion of this aspect of Irenaeus' theology in G. Wingren, *Man and the Incarnation: A Study in the Biblical Theology of Irenaeus* (Philadelphia: Muhlenberg, 1959), pp. 26-38.

36. *Adv. haer.* 3.9.3 (ANF, 1:423).

37. *Ibid.* 3.5.2 (ANF, 1:418).

38. *Ibid.* 3.18.6 (ANF, 1:447-48). There are literally dozens of texts in which Irenaeus expresses similar ideas.

39. The classical discussion of Irenaeus' understanding of the work of Christ is in G. Aulén, *Christus Victor: An Historical Study of the Three Main Types of the Idea of the Atonement* (New York: Macmillan, 1957). The reader will note that the three types of the idea of the atonement which Aulén discusses roughly correspond to the three types of theology discussed here. Indeed, Aulén's work is like a probe into a particular aspect of theology which seems to confirm much of the thesis of this essay.

40. *Ibid.* 5.16.2.

41. This is the term employed in Ephesians 1:10, which the RSV translates "to unite." A better translation is the Jerusalem Bible's: "Bring everything together under Christ, as head."

42. *Adv. haer.* 2.22.4; *Epid.* 34, 37-38.

43. *Adv. haer.* 5.2.2; 5.14.2; *Epid.* 6.

44. *Adv. haer.* 3.19.3.

45. *Ibid.* 3.18.1.

46. The well-known passage of Paul in II Cor. 5:17, usually interpreted in individualistic terms, may well have this further, cosmic meaning. Literally, Paul does not say that if anyone is in Christ "he is a new creature" (KJV) or "he is a new creation." Paul actually says, "If anyone is in Christ, a new creation."

47. *Ibid.* 3.16.6 (ANF, 1:443).

48. *Ibid.* 3.19.1 (ANF, 1:448-49).

49. *Ibid.* 3.19.3 (ANF, 1:449).

50. *Ibid.* 3.17.2 (ANF, 1:445): "For our bodies have received unity among themselves by means of that laver which leads to incorruption; but our souls, by means of the Spirit."

51. This nourishment is not purely spiritual, since it also affects the body. "How can they say that the flesh, which is nourished with the body of the Lord and with His blood, goes to corruption?" *Ibid.* 4.18.5 (ANF, 1:486). The context shows that Irenaeus is referring here to communion. Cf. *Ibid.* 5. 2.2.

52. *Ibid.* 2. 18. 3 (ANF, 1:399): "not only in the present world, but also in that which is to come, so that God should for ever teach, and man should for ever learn the things taught him." Cf. *Ibid.* 4.11.2; 4.28.4.

53. *Ibid.* 4 *praef.* (ANF, 1:463): "There is none other called God by the Scriptures except the Father of all, and the Son, *and those who possess the adoption*" (italics mine).

Ibid. 4.28.4 (ANF, 1:552): "For we cast blame upon Him, because we have not been made gods from the beginning, but at first merely men, and then at length gods." See also: 3.6.1; 3.20.2; 5. *praef.*

54. *Ibid.* 5.32.1 (ANF, 1:561).

55. *Ibid.*

56. Quoted by Irenaeus, *Adv. haer.* 5.33.3. See *History* 1:82-83.

57. *Ibid.* 2.28.3 (ANF, 1:400): "We hope to be receiving ever more and more from God, and to learn from Him, because He is good, and possesses boundless riches, a kingdom without end, and instruction that can never be exhausted."

Notes to Chapter IV

1. *Adv. haer.* 3.11.8.

2. "It ought to be clearly seen to whom belongs the possession of the Scriptures, that none may be admitted to the use thereof who has no title to the privilege." *Praes.* 15 (ANF, 3:250).

3. Actually, Tertullian's argument is thoroughly and consciously based on the Roman legal principle of *"praescriptio longe tempore,"* according to which the undisputed possession of a property or a right for a certain amount of time amounts to an acknowledgment of that property or right. Cf. D. Michaelides, *Foi, Ecriture et tradition: Les Praescriptiones chez Tertullian* (Paris: Editions Aubier-Montague, 1969), pp. 128-31.

4. See J.E.L. Van Der Geest, *Le Christ et l'Ancien Testament chez Tertullien: Recherche terminologique* (Nijmegen: Dekker & Ven de Vegt, 1972), pp. 16-24.

5. *Webster's Third International Dictionary.*

6. Other names Tertullian gives to Scripture and which have legal connotations: *testamentum, lex, literae.* See Van Der Geest, *Le Christ,* pp. 24-39.

7. *Ibid.,* pp. 99-131.

8. At this point, it may be significant to point out that Tertullian, as well as most of the early Christian writers who appealed to prophecy, most often did so to prove the continuity between Jesus and the faith and religion of the Hebrew Scriptures, rather than to prove the divinity of Jesus, as is usually the case today.

9. A rapid survey of his use of the books of Kings and Chronicles in *Against Marcion* will yield a number of passing references, most to the cycles of Elijah and Elisha. Many of these references are mere moral allusions, in which the action of the prophet is used as an example for contemporary behavior. Several remind us of the typological interpretation we shall discuss under Type C (see, for instance, *Adv. Marc.* 4.24). A clear case of typological interpretation occurs in *Adv. Jud.* 13, but this probably is not a genuine writing of Tertullian.

10. *Figura* is the Latin word with which Tertullian translates the Greek "typos." Therefore it appears most often in his writing when he is making use of typological hermeneutics, which he derives from earlier authors such as Justin and Irenaeus. Irenaeus would agree with Tertullian that, once the

reality has come, the figure or type is seen as such. But he would not interpret this as meaning that we are now under a new law.

11. See, for instance, his discussion of the law of divorce in *Adv. Marc.* 4.34.

12. Two excellent studies: Richard P. Hanson, *Allegory and Event: A Study of the Sources and Significance of Origen's Interpretation of Scripture* (London: SCM, 1959) and H. de Lubac, *Histoire et Esprit: L'intelligence de l'Écriture d'après Origène* (Paris: Aubier, 1950). A more recent and much briefer treatment: Jack B. Rogers and Donald K. McKim, *The Authority and Interpretation of the Bible* (San Francisco: Harper & Row, 1979), pp. 11-16.

13. See *De princ.* 4.1.11.

14. The value of the literal meaning, however, must not be underestimated, for there are many who are not capable or ready to ascend to the higher meanings, for whom a more sophisticated discourse would be worthless. "For our prophets, and Jesus Himself, and His apostles, were careful to adopt a style of address which should not merely convey truth, but which should be fitted to gain over the multitude, until each one, attracted and led onwards, should ascend as far as he could towards the comprehension of those mysteries which are contained in these apparently simple words." *Adv. Cel.* 6.2 (ANF, 4:573).

15. *De princ.* 4.1.8.

16. Commenting on a passage from Origen's *Commentary on John* in which he implies that there are rules for proper allegorical interpretation, Hanson rightly says that "in fact no such rules can be deduced in Origen's application of allegory. His use of it breaks all rules and is unchartably allegoric." *Allegory and Event*, p. 245.

17. See a brief discussion of this subject, with concrete examples, in R. M. Grant, *The Earliest Lives of Jesus* (London: SPCK, 1961), pp. 45-46. Origen himself criticized his pagan adversaries for accepting allegorical interpretations of their own literature but not of Scripture. "If, then, they peruse the Theogonies of the Greeks, and the stories about the twelve gods, they impart them an air of dignity, by investing them with an allegorical signification; but when they wish to throw contempt upon our biblical narratives, they assert that they are fables, clumsily invented for infant children!" *Contra Cel.* 4.44 (ANF, 4:516).

18. On the connection between Philo and Clement at the point of hermeneutics, see C. Mondésert, *Clement d'Alexandrie: Introduction à l'étude de sa pensée religieuse à partir de l'Ecriture* (Paris: Aubier, 1944), pp. 163-83.

19. *Contra Cel.* 7.22 (ANF, 4:619-20).

20. *Allegory and Event*, p. 248. On the other hand, as Hanson also acknowledges (p. 371), Origen did not allow his Platonism to carry him too far from Christian orthodoxy. He held fast to such doctrines as the ultimate significance of Jesus and the resurrection of the body, though they did not fit well with his Platonic presuppositions.

In the preface to *De principiis* (which may have been doctored by his translator Rufinus) he outlined the teachings of the church, distinguishing elements about which there was no room for doubt from those on which the tradition allowed for further inquiry; "that alone is to be accepted as truth which differs in no respect from ecclesiastical and apostolical tradition" (ANF, 4:239).

21. *Adv. haer.* 4.14.2 (ANF, 1:479). Italics are mine.

22. See A. Benoit, *Saint Irenée: Introduction à l'étude de sa théologie* (Paris: Presses Universitaires de France, 1960), pp. 219-27; Rowan A. Greer, in James L. Kugel and Rowan A. Greer, *Early Biblical Interpretation* (Philadelphia: Westminister, 1986), pp. 165-68.

23. This can be clearly seen in the very structure of Irenaeus' *Proof of the Apostolic Preaching* (or *Epideixis*), where much of the outline itself—particularly in the early chapters—follows the history of God's dealings with humankind. This is also one of the values of Gustav Wingren's *Man and the Incarnation: A Study in the Biblical Theology of Irenaeus* (Philadelphia: Muhlenberg, 1959), which follows the same order in expounding Irenaeus' theology.

24. *Adv. haer.* 4.20.7 (ANF, 1:489). The passage continues along the same lines, declaring that the Son has "revealed God to men through many dispensations" and that this was done "that man might be disciplined beforehand and previously exercised for a reception into that glory which shall afterwards be revealed in those who love God."

25. In *Adv. haer.* 2.27.2 (ANF, 1:398), Irenaeus complains about the heretics—"Every one of them imagines, by means of their obscure interpretations of the parables, that he has found out a God of his own"—and then goes on to affirm (*Adv. haer.* 2.28.3; ANF, 1:400) that "the parables shall harmonize with those passages which are perfectly plain; and those statements the meaning of which is clear, shall serve to explain the parables."

26. The examples are so many that it is impossible to cite them all here. See, for instance, I Cor. 10:1-4. In Gal. 4:24, there is a semantic problem, in that what Paul calls an "allegory" is what we now call a typology. Also in the cases where the New Testament uses prophecies, it is possible to see such use as typological rather than merely "prophetic" in the sense of foretelling the future.

For instance, when Matthew 2:15 declares that the flight into Egypt "was to fulfil what the Lord had spoken by the prophet, 'Out of Egypt have I called my son,' " is this "prophetic" interpretation, in the sense that Matthew believes that the text in Hosea 11:1 was nothing but a prediction of Jesus' exile? Or is it rather typological, in the sense that what appears in Exodus 4:22 and in Hosea is a pattern that finds its culmination ("fulfillment") in Jesus?

27. *Dial.* 114.1. See *History*, 1:105-6, especially n. 48.

28. *Adv. haer.* 4.20.12 (ANF, 1:492). Cf. *Adv. haer.* 4.14.3; 4.19.1.

29. It is failure to see this fundamental difference between allegory and typology that leads John Lawson to fault Irenaeus for excessive allegorization of Scripture: *The Biblical Theology of Saint Irenaeus* (London: Epworth, 1948), p. 83.

30. *Adv. hear.* 4.14.3 (ANF, 1:479).

31. As Hanson has said, "It would be quite inaccurate to suggest that Origen abandoned traditional Christian typology in his exegesis." *Allegory and Event*, p. 253. He then goes on to give a number of examples.

32. See, for instance, *Adv. haer.* 5.8.4.

Notes to Chapter V

1. In recent years, there have been numerous attempts to fill this gap in historical research. The Society of Biblical Literature and the American

Academy of Religion have organized a Working Group on the Social World of Early Christianity. Much work on New Testament communities has been done along these lines. See W. A. Meeks, *The First Urban Christians: The Social World of the Apostle Paul* (New Haven: Yale University Press, 1983), and the bibliography it contains. More popular, but also attempting to summarize the most relevant findings, is J. E. Stambaugh and D. L. Balch, *The New Testament in Its Social Environment* (Philadelphia: Westminster, 1986).

In any case, the difficulty regarding our lack of sources remains, for as Ramsay MacMullen says, "Christianity after New Testament times is presented to us almost exclusively in pages addressed to upper-class readers," *Christianizing the Roman Empire:* A.D. *100–400* (New Haven: Yale University Press, 1984). This quote continues with an assertion that is much more debatable: "And they preferred to keep a good distance between themselves and their inferiors."

2. *Contra Cel.* 3.55 (ANF, 4:486).

3. *Or. ad Graec.* 1.

4. Josephus, *Ant.* 18.6.3.

5. David L. Mealand, "Philo of Alexandria'a Attitude to Riches," *ZntW*, LXIX (1978), p. 264. This article contains a wealth of information and references which I have found useful for the present essay.

6. C. Bigg, *The Christian Platonists of Alexandria* (Oxford: Clarendon, 1886), p. 41.

7. *Contra Cel.* 1.8, 10, 21; 2.60; 3.34, 48, 79; 4.54, 75; 5.5.

8. *Dial.* 3; *Paneg.* 6.

9. *Strom.* 1. 20.

10. *Ibid.* 5. 71.

11. Bigg, *Christian Platonists*, p. 86.

12. R. B. Tollinton, *Alexandrine Teaching on the Universe* (New York: Macmillan, 1932), p. 159.

13. Perpetua is said to be of noble birth and solid education ("*honeste nata, liberaliter instituta, matronaliter nupta*"). *Passio SS. Perp. et Fel.* 2.

14. *De cultu fem.* 2.10. On the other hand, he declared that Jesus defended the poor and condemned the rich (*De pat.* 7); and that the rich would have more difficulty than others at the time of trial (*De cultu fem.* 13).

15. Tertullian, *De fuga in pers.* 12.

16. *De cultu fem.* 1.9.

17. Tertullian, *Apol.* 2,7; Minucius Felix, *Oct.* 9.

18. *Apol.* 10.

19. One must keep in mind that in the ancient world there was a marked difference between social status and economic class. In the case of Lyon, A.H.M. Jones, "The Economic Life of the Towns of the Roman Empire," *Recueils da la Societé Jean Bodin* (1955), pp. 182-83, has shown that among the merchants and entrepreneurs of Lyon there were foreigners and freedmen, but none having even the title of citizenship, much less aristocratic standing. Since the known names of Christians in the area at that time are mostly Greek, it would appear that, if any had any standing in the community, this must have been a matter of wealth rather than of social status.

20. Eusebius, *H. E.* 5.1.10.

21. Stambaugh and Balch, *The New Testament*, p. 151.

22. Meeks, *Urban Christians*, p. 73.
23. *Adv. haer.* 3.25.3 (ANF, 1:459).
24. *Adv. haer.* 5.24.2 (ANF, 1:552).

Notes to Chapter VI

1. See N. O. King, *The Emperor Theodosius and the Establishment of Christianity* (London: SCM, 1961); A. Momigliano, ed., *Paganism and Christianity in the Fourth Century* (Oxford: Clarendon, 1963).

2. *Adv. haer.* 2.19.8 (ANF, 1:387).

3. In *A History of Christian Thought*, I have discussed Eusebius only in passing. There is more about him in my later work, *The Story of Christianity* (San Francisco: Harper & Row, 1984), 1:129-35.

4. This statement, however, needs to be balanced by a recognition of the influence of Type C in Eusebius: "Eusebius, standing at Caesarea midway between Antioch and Alexandria, tempered his admiration of Origen with a reverence for the observed fact which is wholly Antiochene, and nowhere is this more apparent than in his historical writing. . . . He saw human history as exhibiting a pattern in which the patriarchal age of faith was recapitulated in the Christian age of grace, the two ages being separated by the intervening Mosaic age of Law. The age of the last things had begun with Christ and had achieved its consummation in the conversion to Christianity of the empire under Constantine." D. S. Wallace-Hadrill, *Christian Antioch: A Study of Early Christian Thought in the East* (Cambridge: University Press, 1982), pp. 52-53.

5. In Pliny's correspondence with Trajan—the same correspondence that includes the well-known data about Christians in Bithynia—there is a case where Pliny had suggested to Trajan the formation of a voluntary society of firefighters. Trajan responded that it was precisely such societies that had created previous disturbances in Bithynia, and that such groups, no matter what their purpose, eventually became political movements. *Ep.* 10.34.

6. As Celsus would put it, "If all were to do the same as you, there would be nothing to prevent his {the king's} being left in utter solitude and desertion, and the affairs of the earth would fall into the hands of the wildest and most lawless barbarians." In Origen, *Contra Cel.* 8.68 (ANF, 4:665).

7. Robert L. Wilken, *The Christians as the Roman Saw Them* (New Haven: Yale University Press, 1984), p. 119.

8. The statement of Norman K. Gottwald regarding biblical scholars is just as true regarding historians: "Biblical scholars from the Renaissance to the bourgeois revolutions of the seventeenth through the nineteenth centuries were generally the intellectual adjuncts of monarchic, aristocratic, or clerical class interests. Increasingly in the nineteenth century, they became one functional group among many academicians and intellectuals who shared in the bourgeois revolutions against monarchic and aristocratic domination. . . . By and large the position of biblical scholars, as a professional and intellectual elite, was oppositional both toward the declining monarchies and aristocracies

and toward the rising underclasses of the industrial proletariat and, later, the peasantry. In contrast to the formerly dominant classes they were liberative and progressive, but toward the classes below them they were conservative and reactionary." *The Tribes of Yahweh: A Sociology of the Religion of Liberated Israel, 1250-1050 B.C.E.* (Maryknoll, N.Y.: Orbis, 1979), p. 10.

9. See the note to that effect in NPNF, 2nd series, 1:154. Cf. *H. E.* 3.39.13.

10. *H. E.* 3.39.13.

11. *Ibid.* 10.4.

12. *History,* 1:248-52.

13. *Ibid.,* 1:269-70, 274-75, 338-39.

14. *Ibid.,* 1:353-67.

15. See *Ibid.,* 1:263-65.

16. *Ibid.,* 1:335-80; 2:76-91.

17. "To put it as a wild generalisation which amounts almost to a parody, we may say that in certain aspects the Byzantine thinking about God and the Emperor had three noxious end-products (this is not to mention the many excellent results). Firstly, Christian victory came to be thought of as the Emperor's success in the field; secondly, thinking about Christ became too much influenced by thinking about the Emperor; thirdly, the Emperor became too closely aligned with God to be devoid of all hint of blasphemy." N. Q. King, *"There's such Divinity Doth Hedge a King": Studies in Ruler Cult and the Religion of Some Late Fourth-Century Byzantine Monuments* (Nashville: Thomas Nelson, 1960), p. 19.

18. *History,* 1:368-80; 2:76-91.

19. *History,* 2:15-55.

20. For a basic bibliography on the nature and content of Augustine's conversion, see *History,* 2:23, n. 15.

21. *Conf.* 7.20.

22. "To a man like Augustine all our talk about progress, crisis, and world order would have seemed insignificant; for, from the Christian point of view, there is only one progress: the advance toward an ever sharper distinction between faith and unbelief, Christ and Antichrist; these are the only two crises of real significance: Eden and Calvary." Karl Löwith, *Meaning in History* (Chicago: University of Chicago, 1949), p. 172.

23. Gerhart B. Lardner, *The Idea of Reform: Its Impact on Christian Thought and Action in the Age of the Fathers* (Cambridge: Harvard University Press, 1959), p. 160, n. 22.

24. *Ench.* 104; *De Gen. ad litt.* 6.20-23.

25. *History,* 2:63-65.

26. González, *Mañana: Christian Theology from a Hispanic Perspective* (Nashville: Abingdon Press), forthcoming.

27. *Ench.* 29.

28. *De dono persev.* 12.28.

29. *De nat. et grat.* 30.33.

30. See W.H.C. Frend, *The Donatist Church: A Movement of Protest in Roman North Africa* (Oxford: Clarendon, 1952).

31. In a chapter appropriately titled "Pax Romana, Endless War," Pierre Hubac has summarized the history of North Africa from the time of the Punic wars to the Germanic invasions: "From the year 111 B.C. to 417 A.D.., during 528

years, there would be endless war. And the nomad would not be alone against the Roman. All that for whatever reason are Punic in appearance will be banded against the Roman. The despoiled sedentaries, reduced to serfdom, will make common cause with the nomads, their former foes. All against Rome, for five centuries and a half." *Carthage* (Paris: Bellenand, 1952), p. 236.

32. See *History,* 2:26-29; *Story,* 1:151-57.

Notes to Chapter VII

1. *History,* 2:71-74.

2. *Ibid.,* 1:229-32.

3. *Ibid.,* 1:235.

4. *Ibid.,* 2:26-29

5. Caesarius of Arles (in PL as Pseudo-Augustine), *Serm.* 256; 257.3. Isidore of Seville, *De off.* 2. 9. On the other hand, see Caesarius, *Serm.* 249.6; 258.2.

6. E. Amman, "Pénitence: Les Ve et VIe siècles," DTC, 12:835-36.

7. See, for instance, the A.D. 589 decree of the Council of Toledo: "It has come to our attention that, in certain churches in Spain, there are those who make penance for their sins, not according to the canons, but in their own sickening way, so that whenever they sin they go to seek reconciliation from mere priests. In order to destroy such execrable presumption, the holy council commands that penance be administered according to the canonical forms of the ancients." (PL, 34:353).

8. See G. LeBas, "Pénitentiels," DTC, 12: 1160-79.

9. Canon 21: "All the faithful of either sex who have reached the age of discretion must confess their faults to their own priests at least once a year, fulfil to the best of their ability the penance imposed, and reverently partake of the sacrament of the eucharist, at least on Easter, unless their priest has good reason to postpone the taking of the sacrament. Those who disobey will be excluded from the church; and when they die they will not be granted Christian burial.

10. See Mary Flowers Braswell, *The Medieval Sinner: Characterization and Confession in the Literature of the English Middle Ages* (London: Associated University Presses, 1983).

11. *De civ. Dei* 21.13, 24, 26; *De Gen. contra Manich.* 20.30.

12. *Dial.* 4.39, 55; *Moral.* 15. 29.

13. The doctrine of purgatory was one of the points at issue between East and West at the time of the Council. The West insisted on its position and imposed a compromise on the East, which acquiesced for political reasons. In the decree of the Council, the fires of purgatory are called "purifying or expiating." The second term expresses the commonly held view in the West, while the first could be interpreted in the sense of Origen's doctrine.

14. See, for instance, Albertus Magnus, *In IV Sent.* 4.2.16.

15. This is seen in the story of the monk Justus, whom Gregory had condemned for owning private property. After the monk's death, Gregory relented and ordered that thirty masses be said for his soul. According to Gregory's account, a fellow monk received word from Justus that he was now

out of purgatory and had been admitted to heaven. *Dial.* 6. 55. Thereafter such masses for the dead were sometimes called "Gregorian masses."

16. *De pat.* 13; *De cult. fem.* 1.1.

17. *De fug. saec.* 7.44.

18. *Comm. in Ps.* 53.12; 129.9.

19. 2.6.

20. This is one more example of the manner in which a Type A theology —the human predicament is that we owe a debt to God—is combined with elements from Type B—the contrast between the infinite God and human finitude. The result, however, is to make Type A even more onerous.

21. *History,* 2:130-37.

22. *De div. nat.* 1.26.

23. *History,* 2:93-96.

24. *Ibid.,* 2:167-74.

Notes to Chapter VIII

1. *History,* 3:29-34.

2. "By the grace of God, I have learned to know a great deal about Satan." Quoted by Paul Althaus, *The Theology of Martin Luther* (Philadelphia: Fortress, 1966), p. 162.

3. *History,* 3:55-57.

4. On this point, compare Althaus, *Theology,* pp. 203-23, and G. Aulén, *Christus Victor: An Historical Study of the Three Main Types of the Idea of the Atonement* (New York: Macmillan, 1957), pp. 101-22.

5. See Jaroslav Pelikan, *Luther the Expositor: Introduction to the Reformer's Exegetical Writings* (Saint Louis: Concordia, 1959), pp. 48-70.

6. "We must therefore beware of those who have reduced the power of baptism to such small and slender dimensions that, while they say grace is inpoured in it, they maintain that afterwards it is poured out again through sin, and that one must reach heaven by another way, as if baptism had now become entirely useless. . . . Baptism never becomes useless, unless you despair and refuse to return to its salvation. You may indeed wander away from the sign for a time, but the sign is not therefore useless. . . . We are therefore never without the sign of baptism nor without the thing that it signifies. Indeed, we need continually to be baptized more and more, until we fulfill the sign perfectly at the last day." *The Babylonian Captivity of the Church* (LW, 36:69).

7. See Catherine L. Gunsalus, *The Place of the Concept* felix culpa *in Christian Doctrine.* Dissertation, Boston University, 1965, pp. 88-90.

8. "That one article concerning justification even by itself creates true theologians." *The Disputation Concerning Justification* (LW, 34:157).

9. *History,* 3:68-69.

10. *Preface to the Latin Writings* (LW, 34:337).

11. The most remarkable exception is the *Barmen Declaration,* as much Reformed as it is Lutheran.

12. *History,* 3:70-85.

13. *Ibid.,* 3:53-58.

14. *Inst.* 2.17.4-5.

15. Perhaps the most remarkable Type C insight in Calvin, one the Calvinists soon lost, was the way he related communion with the risen Christ and the Kingdom. On this point, most later Calvinists returned to the medieval emphasis on the cross and repentance for our sins. See *Inst.* 4.17.29, 31-32.

16. *History,* 3:86-98.

17. See Ugo Gastaldi, *Storia dell'anabattismo dalle origini a Munster, 152-1535* (Torino: Editrice Claudiana, 1972), in which this theme is shown to appear quite independently in various parts of Europe.

18. *History,* 3:248-65.

19. *Ibid.,* 3:279-88, 290-99. For a fuller discussion on the specific subject of biblical interpretation, see also Jack B. Rogers and Donald K. McKim, *The Authority and Interpretation of the Bible* (San Francisco: Harper & Row, 1979), pp. 172-379.

20. *History,* 3:261-63.

21. *Ibid.,* 3:321-26.

22. *Ibid.,* 3:328-32.

23. *Ibid.,* 3:332-35.

24. *Ibid.,* 3:335-38.

25. At this point, it may be well to point out that many of the Deists claimed that true Christianity agreed with universal natural religion and that Judaism's insistence on the importance of the history of a particular people was a case of superstition. In this they followed the lead of Kant, who in *Religion Within the Limits of Reason Alone* (New York: Harper & Brothers, 1960), pp. 116-17, declared, "It is evident that the Jewish faith stands in no essential connection whatever, *i.e.,* in no unity of concepts, with this ecclesiastical faith whose history we wish to consider. . . . Judaism is really not a religion at all but merely a union of a number of people who, since they belonged to a particular stock, formed themselves into a commonwealth under purely political laws. . . . Judaism fell so far short of constituting an era suited to the requirements of the church universal, or of setting up this universal church itself during its time, as actually to exclude from its communion the entire human race, on the ground that it was a special people chosen by God for Himself—[an exclusiveness] which showed enmity toward all other peoples and which, therefore, evoked the enmity of all." This contraposition between Christianity and Judaism, supposedly based on purely rational considerations, lay at the root of much anti-Jewish feeling and much Jewish suffering.

26. *History,* 3:302-6.

27. *Ibid.,* 3:206-16.

28. *Ibid.,* 3:279-88.

29. Christianity is essentially a social religion; and . . . to turn it into a solitary one is to destroy it." *Sermon* 24.5 (*Works,* 5:296).

30. *History,* 3:362-64.

31. *History,* 3:377-82.

32. *Ibid.,* 3:374-77.

33. *What is Christianity?* (New York: Harper Torchbooks, 1957), p. 51. (First published in German in 1900.)

34. *Ibid.,* p. 56.

35. See in this regard the judgment of Karl Barth, that Ritschl's view of the

Christian life is "the very epitome of the national-liberal German bourgeois of the age of Bismark." *From Rousseau to Ritschl* (London: SCM, 1959), p. 392. Also quoted in *History,* 3:377.

36. Walter Rauschenbusch, *Christianity and the Social Crisis* (New York: Macmillan, 1919), p. 108.

37. "It is an essential doctrine of the Word of God and our standards that Christ offered up Himself a sacrifice to satisfy Divine Justice and to reconcile us to God." William Jennings Bryan, *Orthodox Christianity versus Modernism,* quoted in Fred Berthold, et al., eds., *Basic Sources of the Judaeo-Christian Tradition* (Englewood Cliffs, N.J.: Prentice-Hall, 1962), p. 408.

38. See *History,* 2:296-97.

39. *History,* 3:457-59.

40. Ed. Carl E. Braaten (New York: Harper & Row, 1968).

41. *Systematic Theology,* Vol. 1 (Chicago: University Press, 1951), p. 205.

42. *Ibid.,* Vol. 2 (Chicago: University Press, 1957), pp. 29-44.

43. *History,* 3:440-45.

44. *Kerygma and Myth* (New York: Harper & Brothers, 1961), p. 35.

Notes to Chapter IX

1. These and other statistics that show similar trends may be found in David K. Barrett, ed., *World Christian Encyclopaedia* (Nairobi: Oxford University Press, 1982), "global tables" No. 18 and 19.

2. In Stephen Neill, ed., *Twentieth Century Christianity* (New York: Doubleday, 1962), p. 8.

3. See *In Defense of Creation,* p. 53.

4. *Bulletin of Atomic Scientists,* February 1985, p. 12. Quoted by Luis N. Rivera Pagán, "Idolatría nuclear y paz en el mundo: breves reflexiones teológicas," *Apuntes* 7:1987, p. 77.

5. *History,* 3:432-40.

6. See "Das erste Gebot als theologisches Axiom," *Zwischen den Zeiten,* 12 (1933), especially p. 308. See also his response to Emil Brunner: *Nein! Antwort an Emil Brunner, Theologische Existenz heute,* No. 14.

7. *The Humanity of God* (Richmond: John Knox, 1960), pp. 45-46.

8. *Ibid.,* p. 47.

9. *History,* 3:447-49.

10. *Ibid.,* 3:449.

11. *Ibid.,* 3:451-52.

12. *Ibid.,* 3:452-55.

13. *Das Prinzip Hoffnung* (Frankfort: Suhrkamp, 1959). English trans., *The Principle of Hope* (Cambridge: M.I.T. Press, 1982).

14. *History,* 3:460-68; *Story,* 2:345-59.

15. *The Documents of Vatican II,* "The Church in the Modern World," 38.

16. See a series of quotes to this effect from Latin American, black, and feminist theologians in Justo L. González and Catherine G. González, *Liberation Preaching: The Pulpit and the Oppressed* (Nashville: Abingdon Press, 1980), pp. 20-21.

17. *History,* 1:229-35. Note there that Hippolytus followed Irenaeus in his

understanding of Christ's work as "recapitulation," and in his eschatology. However, Hippolytus' moral rigorism, which eventually led him to break with the rest of the church in Rome, is more akin to Type A. It is significant that by this time both he and his opponent Callistus seem to be arguing within the parameters of Type A.

18. *Baptism, Eucharist and Ministry* (Geneva: World Council of Churches, 1982), p. 6.

19. *A Service of Baptism, Confirmation, and Renewal* (Nashville: United Methodist Publishing House, 1976), p. 15.

20. *Holy Baptism and Services for the Renewal of Baptism,* Supplemental Liturgical Resources No. 2 (Philadelphia: Westminster, 1985), p. 28.

Index

179